Architectural Guide
Mexico City

Architectural Guide
Mexico City

Sarah Zahradnik

With contributions by Adlai Pulido
and Inka Humann

DOM
publishers

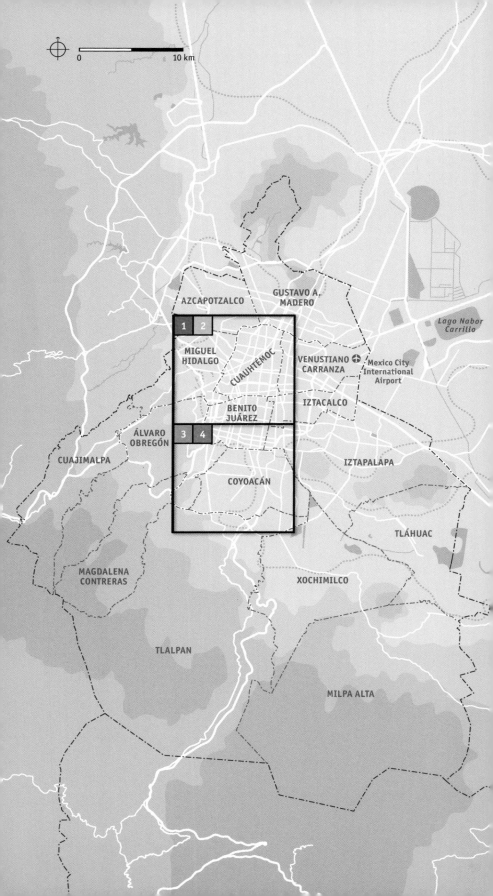

Contents

030 Reforma 222

031 BMV (Stock Exchange)

017 Monumento a la Independencia

The Paseo de la Reforma is not only one of the most important axis of the city, but its primary green belt as well

035 Torre Mayor

Parque de Chapultepec

047 Krystal Grand Reforma Uno

027 Monumento a la Revolución

The tallest buildings in Mexico City flank the Paseo de la Reforma
and some of the most important avenues nearby

030 Reforma 222

031 BMV (Stock Exchange)

Parque de Chapultepec

View of Cuauhtémoc from the Castillo de Chapultepec. The Paseo de la Reforma goes through the park before becoming one of the most important axis of the city

031 BMV (Stock Exchange)

035 Torre Mayor

017 Monumento a la Independencia

046 Torre BBVA Bancomer

Altar a la Patria

Paseo de la Reforma on a Sunday morning (2014)

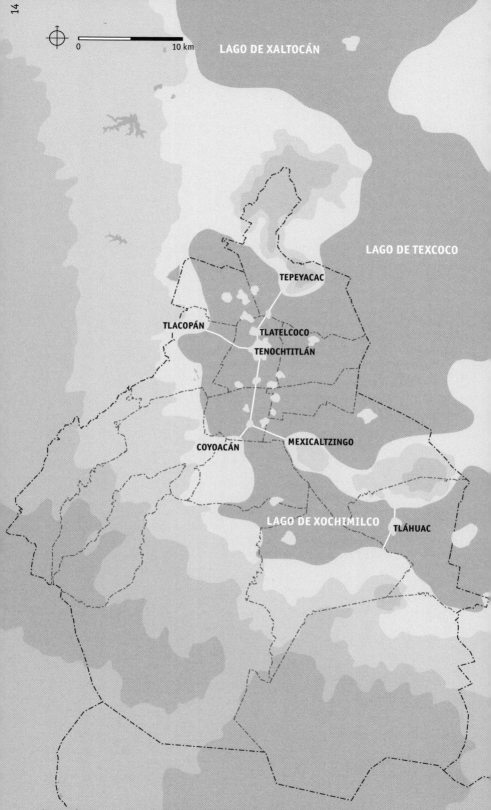

0   10 km

LAGO DE XALTOCÁN

LAGO DE TEXCOCO

TEPEYACAC

TLACOPÁN

TLATELCOCO

TENOCHTITLÁN

COYOACÁN   MEXICALTZINGO

LAGO DE XOCHIMILCO   TLÁHUAC

Approximate overlay of Tenochtitlán and Lake Texcoco (sixteenth century)
on today's Mexico City

From Islet to Megalopolis

Adlai Pulido

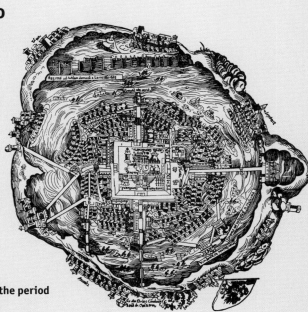

Tenochtitlán during the period of the conquistadors

Islet. n.
A very small island, an area of land completely surrounded by water but not large enough to be called a continent.

Megalopolis. n.
A very large city. An urban region consisting of several large cities and suburbs that adjoin one other.

About 800 years ago, what is now known today as Mexico City was a lake, inhabited by a pre-Hispanic culture: the Aztecs. With very precise organisation and hierarchical orders, they developed the first traces of the city. Within this lake area, sits an island of approximately 80 x 100 m. The city of Tenochtitlán was built on a grid plan with a centre for worshipping the gods. This urban layout, with its large and narrow streets, corresponded to the city's strategic access. Aqueducts brought fresh water from distant areas and an intricate drainage system maintained the municipality's salubrity. This progress was highly innovative for the period itself, the Aztecs were the inventive engineers of their period; they were the most prolific civilisation that existed in the Prehispanic age. Unfortunately, this culture only existed for 200 years.

Bird's-eye view of Tenochtitlán, thirteenth century

Fundación Tenochtitlán (Foundation of Tenochtitlán), by Roberto Cueva del Río

View over the historic centre of México City in the eighteenth century

In 1512, with the discovery of America and a few years later, in 1521, with the arrival of the Spanish conquistadors, there were drastic changes made in the city; most of the traditional pyramidal temples were partially and entirely destroyed, and on top of them were built new ceremonial centres, government buildings and other constructions, which would implant the viceroyalty of New Spain completely.

The conquest introduced a completely different way of thinking. Although the layout of the city was preserved, new urbanisation criteria appeared: building systems, and the expansion of the city itself were changed. While the first inhabitants understood that they were building on a lake, the latter ignored this geographical element and began to densify the city with buildings, which gradually took over the lake. All that was left of the urban grid were the strategic access points, implemented during the foundation of Tenochtitlán. By 1800, the city of Mexico had grown gradually and what started as an island could now be defined as an urban area. The lake was reduced to small bodies of water. Some rivers still existed but no longer in the downtown area. The city centre was occupied by robust constructions, which ended up occupying the lakeside space and shaped the image of today's downtown, and other neighbourhoods of the city where urban growth was more intensive.

The independence of Mexico took place in the early nineteenth century, and its effects were radical for the growth of the city; the so-called City of Palaces, continued to expand under this new regime, which started forming districts and neighbourhoods that each had a particular characteristic. The viceroyal aesthetics began to mix with other styles, amongst them, the French, as a symbol of modernity and thus the city continued its rapidly accelerating growth, already reaching a population of 0.7 million by the early 1900s.

Together with the introduction of the railway, urban growth began to intensify with the arrival of private cars and mass transit. By the mid-twentieth century, the urban population grew from 3.1 to 6.9 million people. This is when the transformation of the city and architecture began to dramatically increase. The effects of the modern movement had arrived in Mexico City with the global developments in transport and communications. Road axis were created, as well as two rings for peripheral automobile circulation. The internal ring is in fact a river that was piped and is used for drainage.

Torre Mayor and Torre Reforma hover over the entrance of the Centre of Digital Culture and Chapultepec park

Aerial view of Mexico City, a recognisable mix of Aztec and European urban patterns

The outer periferical ring, marked the city limits; these have been completely overwhelmed nowadays. The majority of cosmopolitan and modern Mexico City's architectural elements were built and inaugurated from the 1920s to today; a nuance of elements that speak very clearly about Mexican modernity and its history, converting Mexico City into a very unique agglomeration.

Over the passing years, the city has consolidated within the modern Mexico, demonstrating its potential to the world as a developing city; iconic buildings were built, to name a few: the Palace of Fine Arts (1934), the Monument to the Revolution (1938), the first modern housing complex in Mexico: President Miguel Alemán Urban Complex (1947), which leads to many more such as Tlatelolco, the University City of UNAM (1952), the Latinoamericana Tower (1956), the National Museum of Antropology (1964), the Azteca Stadium (1966), and the Basílica of Guadalupe (1976). In addition to this iconic architectural development, came the creation of the *Metro* – public transportation system (1960 to present) – that provides wide access to the contemporary Mexico.

An earthquake in 1985 brought down over 700 buildings in Mexico City. However, even with the intensive damages, the city was quickly rebuilt to be one of today's most densely populated cities in the world, with 8.9 million inhabitants. The urban sprawl has reached its limits and joined the State of Mexico – its neighbouring entity – counting 22 million inhabitants. This might explain why Mexico City cannot be mentioned without thinking of its status as a *megalopolis*. This city's beauty lies in its scale, chaotic quality, vast distances, and particular architecture. The current architectural landscapes of Mexico City portray its cosmopolity and contemporarity, thus characterising it throughout the world as a global capital: a result of hundreds of years of history, culture, and traditions that make this city very unique in its genre.

Museum of the Templo Mayor

Ruins of the old Tenochtitlán

Aerial view over the Cathedral, with the museum of the Templo Mayor behind it

3D illustration of the temple district of Tenochtitlán

003 Catedral de México

Discovery of the ruins of Templo Mayor

Tenochtitlán's main temple complex, the Templo Mayor, was dismantled and the central district of the Spanish colonial city was built on top of it. Templo Mayor was rediscovered in the early twentieth century, but major excavations did not occur until 1978–1982, under the supervision of archeologist Eduardo Matos Moctezuma. Mexico City's *Zócalo* (main square), the Plaza de la Constitución, is located at the site of Tenochtitlán's original central plaza and market, and many of the original *calzadas* (roads) still correspond to modern city streets. The museum of the Templo Mayor was built in 1987 to house the Templo Mayor Project and its finds – a project, which continues to this day. In 1991, the Urban Archeology Program was incorporated as part of the Templo Mayor Project. Its mission is to excavate the oldest area of the city, around the main square. The museum has four floors, three of which are for permanent exhibitions and the fourth houses offices for the director, museum administration, and research staff. Other departments are located in the basement, as well as an auditorium.

Mexico City – more commonly known to the locals as *el D.F.* – is known for its scale and excessively high number of inhabitants, as well as its architecture, culture, and history. This ancient city has been growing since 1325, after the Aztecs discovered it and made it the capital of their empire. Originally based on the relationship to the site's geography, consisting of a lake surrounded by mountains, it was split into four sectors of walkways and canals, which linked the streets and connected them to nearby shores. However, the central lake eventually dried out and the canals were turned into street networks, which is fundamentally what lead to the drastic growth and rapid transformation of the entire city. Nowadays, Mexico City is built around the *Zócalo* (Main Square), the central place from which its grid was built. The city itself though, has numerous central points and is divided into sixteen separate districts: Azcapotzalco, Gustavo A. Madero, Miguel Hidalgo, Cuauhtémoc, Venustiano Carranza, Iztacalco, Benito Juárez, Álvaro Obregón, Cuajimalpa, La Magdalena Contreras, Tlalpan, Coyoacán, Itzapalapa, Tláhuac, Xochimilco and Milpa Alta. During the 1930s, Mexico City was the cultural and political hub of the country, populated by artists and architects, from Juan O'Gorman to Mario Pani, who played fundamental roles in marking a cultural and architectural evolution, particularly with their influential design references to modernity in their residential and urban structures. The post-revolutionary regime dominated the 1920s to the late 1940s and eventually the Mexican capital abandoned its centurys old urban fabric in exchange for a series of institutional and residential districts. The combination of economic, political and demographic factors lead to planned growth and uncontrolled development, which increased during the 1950s and 1960s.

View of colourful buildings and the Iglesia de la Santísima Trinidad, one of the many churches in the historic city centre of Mexico City

The Urban Growth and Transformation of Mexico City

Aerial view of Mexico City centre, with the Paseo de la Reforma clearly marked by the array of skyscrapers that line the avenue

Modern architecture and city planning attempted to address and resolve the issues of overpopulation, with housing and infrastructure. However, informal urbanisation developed outside legal control and professional frameworks, and occurred in illegal sales of land that instigated low rise sprawl. A huge demand for new land and housing was therefore established by this informal urbanisation. Then, came the public administrations restrainment from urban planning around the 1970s, which decided to ignore addressing the rapid growth of what is today's largest metropolitan city in the Western hemisphere. The population and scale of Mexico City barely grew between 1521 and 1900. It was not until after the Mexican Revolution in 1921 that the city began to expand, radically increasing from 3 million inhabitants to over 20 million at the beginning of the twentieth century, and spreading over 250 km^2 as a result of new urban neighbourhoods on the edges. The city was prone to earthquakes in the past, in particular the one of 1985, which destroyed many of Mexico City's buildings,

prompting innovative design techniques for new structures. The Torre Latinoamericana, was structurally designed to withstand earthquakes. Architecture in Mexico consists of a complex combination of colonial and modern influences, but without a specific architectural approach. It can be defined in three main categories, the most important being symbolic and monumental architecture, with profound historical roots. The second category is that of commercial architecture, and the third focuses on the residential. The integration of art and architecture is consistent in modern Mexican architecture. The University Campus of the National Autonomous University of Mexico, designed by Carlos Lazo, Enrique del Moral, and Mario Pani often incorporates the art of Mexican muralists into its architecture. Other examples of murals are Diego Rivera's for the Estadio Olímpico Universitario (by Augusto Pérez Palacios, Jorge Bravo, and Raúl Salinas), and David Alfaro Siqueiros for the Edificio de la Torre de Rectoría by Mario Pani, Enrique del Moral, and Salvador Ortega Flores.

Museo Nacional de Arte

016 Palacio de Correos

Banco de México

014 Palacio de Bellas Artes

View of the east side of the Alameda Central gardens, with the magnificent
Palacio de Bellas Artes at the front

009 Casa de los Azulejos

020 Edificio Guardiola

026 Torre Latinoamericana

022 Edificio La Nacional

Alameda Central

Museo de Arte Popular

040 Museo Memoria y Tolerancia

View of the west side of the Alameda Central gardens, surrounded by many museums and art galleries

Museo Mural Diego Rivera

004 Laboratorio Arte Alameda

Museo Franz Mayer

Alameda Central

001 Plaza de la Constitución

Museo del Templo Mayor

003 Catedral de México

008 Centro Cultural Ex Teresa

011 Antiguo Palacio del Arzobispado

007 Iglesia de Santo Domingo

The Plaza de la Constitución is located in the original site of the Temple District of Tenochtitlán

002 Palacio Nacional

013 El Palacio de Hierro Centro

015 Gran Hotel Ciudad de México

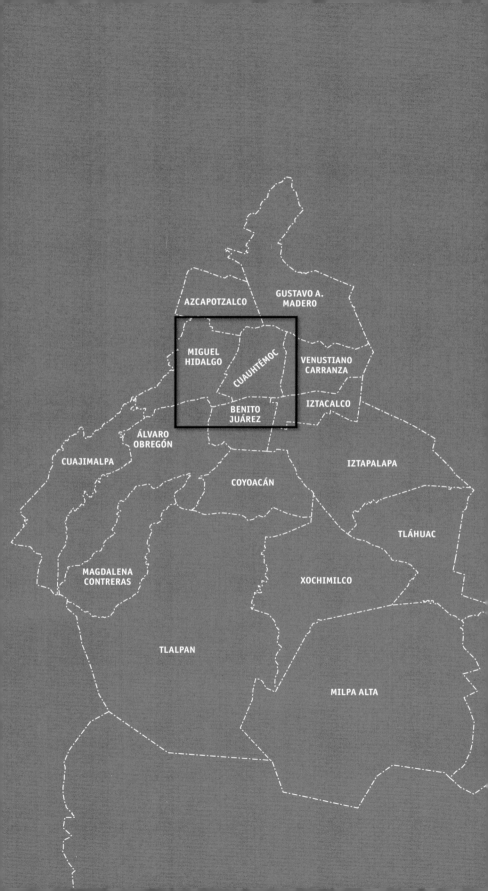

Cuauhtémoc: Historical Centre and Close Landmarks

Cuauhtémoc: Historical Centre and Close Landmarks

The Cuauhtémoc district is located in Mexico City's centre and is the cultural and historic hub of the city. With architectural attractions such as the Palace of Fine Arts, the Monument to the Revolution, and the Angel of Independence, it is the city's most bustling tourist zone. The district's centre point is the main square, the Plaza de la Constitución also known as the *Zócalo*. The square is surrounded by the well-known National Palace and Metropolitan Cathedral. Being the city centre, it is also a highly commercialised area with many skyscrapers and government buildings that draw an average of up to five million people per day. The busiest of the commerial streets are the Avenida de los Insurgentes and the Paseo de la Reforma. The Cuauhtémoc district also houses a wider range of buildings, including many of the city's museums, libraries, and markets.

View of the Plaza de la Constitución, with the Catedral Metropolitana on the left and the Palacio Nacional at the front

Plaza de la Constitución 001 A

Calle Monte de Piedad,
Col. Centro, Cuauhtémoc
Alonso García Bravo, Hernán Cortés
15th century

Palacio Nacional 002 A

Plaza de la Constitución s/n,
Col. Centro, Cuauhtémoc
Rodrigo de Pontocillos, Juan Rodríguez
15th century

Mostly known as the *Zócalo*, the Plaza de la Constitución is situated in the historic city centre. Originally, this space served as the central square for the Aztec Empire, and used to be covered with lush vegetation. Reassigned in the early fifteenth century as Mexico City's main square, it has become a large, bare, open space that is used for performances, exhibitions, and other such events. The Plaza de la Constitución is one of the largest squares in the world with a total of 58,000 m². It is surrounded by the Palacio Nacional, Templo Mayor, and the Metropolitan Catheral. At its centre a huge mast floats the Mexican flag.

The baroque Palacio Nacional was completed during the fifteenth century. The palace's façade is covered with red tezontle rock (exclusive to Mexican construction) and its interior is enclosed by marble walls. It features various courtyards, fountains and gardens. Upon entering the palace's main doors, one arrives in the central courtyard. The second corridor leads you to two of Diego Rivera's famous murals, which depict four centuries of Mexican history. The northern entrance separates the former residence of the late president, Benito Pablo Juárez, which has been converted into a museum.

1

Catedral Metropolitana de la Ciudad de México »   003 A

Plaza de la Constitución s/n,
Col. Centro, Cuauhtémoc
Claudio de Arciniega, Lorenzo Rodríguez,
Juan Miguel de Agüero, Manuel Tolsá,
José Damián Ortiz de Castro
15th to 18th century

Since its original construction, the Catedral Metropolitana de la Ciudad de México has undergone numerous reconstructions, and its soft foundation has caused it to sink. It is the largest cathedral in Latin America and includes various architectural styles. Its façade consists of a central dome, two bell towers and three portals, edged with columns and statues. Inside are five vaults, five altars, a choir area, and sixteen chapels. On the right side of the main entrance is the baroque Tabernacle, which was built in the seventeenth century and is made of red tezontle. The Tabernacle connects to the Metropolitan Cathedral through the Chapel of San Isidro.

Laboratorio Arte Alameda 004 A

Doctor Mora 7,
Col. Centro, Cuauhtémoc
Unknown
16th century

The neoclassical façade, tower and interior of the Laboratorio Arte Alameda have survived the decades. Originally built in the sixteenth century as a Fransiscan Monastery, only the temple and cloister remain in the nowadays Laboratorio Arte Alameda, next to the Alameda Central public garden. The earlier monastery served for public worship until 1934. It was later used as a winery. In 2000 it was remodelled into today's *art laboratory*, which exhibits contemporary art.

Basílica de San José 005 A
y Nuestra Señora
del Sagrado Corazón »

Ayuntamiento 29,
Col. Centro, Cuauhtémoc
Francisco Antonio Guerrero y Torres
1792, 1861

The Basílica de San José y Nuestra Señora del Sagrado Corazón is located just off the San Juan Plaza. It was built in the late eighteenth century and reconstructed, due to an earthquake, in 1858. In 1931 it was declared a historical monument. This yellow basilica resembles the typical Mexican colonial architecture and the façade displays Byzantine bell towers. The inside of this religious building is supported by four baroque columns.

Iglesia de la Santa Veracruz ⤊ 006 A
Calle 2 De Abril 6,
Col. Centro, Cuauhtémoc
Architect unknown
1568, 18th century

The Santa Veracruz Church was built in 1568 and reconstructed in the eighteenth century. It is one of Mexico City's oldest religious establishments. Its façade is covered in tezontle and sandstone. Its structural form contains two portals at the main entrance and a dome. The main entrance is an arched doorway and the top of the exterior walls consist of a series of rounded arches that wrap around the structure. The interior holds one nave enclosed by numerous vaults.

Iglesia de Santo Domingo 007 A
de Guzmán ⤋
Belizario Domínguez s/n,
Col. Centro,Cuauhtémoc
Pedro de Arrieta
1736

This church is the last remnant of the first monastery, established in New Spain. Construction lasted about thirty years, to be completed in 1736. Facing the Santo Domingo Plaza, the baroque exterior consists of tezontle and grey stone materials. Twelve columns surround the main entrance and the building's portal is made up of three bodies of cantera stone. Manuel Tolsá designed the interior altarpiece with neoclassical influences.

Centro Cultural Ex Teresa Arte Actual

Calle Licenciado Verdad 8,
Col. Centro Hostórico, Cuauhtémoc
Luis Vicente Flores
16th century, 1994

The Centro Cultural Ex Teresa Arte Actual is situated in the historic centre. The building itself is made up of two premisses. Formerly the Templo de Santa Teresa la Antigua, it now exhibits contemporary art in the form of installations, performances, and multimedia. The baroque façade and neoclassical interior were built in the sixteenth century. It was then converted into an art musem, in 1994, by the architect Luis Vicente Flores. It is a combination of colonial and contemporary styles, reminiscent of its past and creating a contrast of new functionality to the existing interior spaces. Inside, there are several vaults, high columns, stained glass windows, and a central decorative dome through which natural light passes.

Casa de los Azulejos

Av. Francisco I. Madero,
Col. Centro, Cuauhtémoc
Unknown
15th and 18th centuries

Located just off Guardiola Plaza, this Baroque style house has been used for various purposes. Today, it functions as a department store with a restaurant, bar, and cafeteria. Originally built in the fifteenth century, it underwent a huge reconstruction in the eighteenth century, which included the entire façade being covered in blue and white Talavera tiles. The entire building is combined of two houses. Its decorative façade is the reason behind its name: la Casa de los Azulejos (the House of Tiles). Its façade consists of a large gate, which has been framed by colums and moldings of carved stonework. The walls are also ornate with similar columns, and tiles. A balcony that wraps itself around the entire second level, consists of iron railing. This impressive building features a large interior courtyard with a mosaic-tiled fountain in its centre, surrounded by stone and timber archways. Hallways line the courtyard with large columns reaching all the way up to the second level. A stained glass roof allows this interior space to be lit naturally, and large murals are displayed on two of the interior walls. One of the murals by José Clemente Orozco is situated in the vault of the stairs, which lead to the level above, and adjacent to the flagship restaurant.

Iglesia de la Santísima Trinidad

Calle Emiliano Zapata 60,
Col. Centro, Cuauhtémoc
Ildefonso de Iniesta Bejarano
17th century

This church, its full name being the Templo y Antiguo Hospital de la Santisíma Trinidad (Temple and former Hospital of the Most Holy Trinity) was built during the seventeenth century. This baroque style building was intended to serve as a temple for the neighbouring hospital. The church's interior comprises three naves, vaults, and stained glass windows. The main entrance is accessed through an ornately sculpted wooden door, set in the middle of an intricately sculpted gray stone façade, borded by two massive pillars. A tower sits to the right side of the main portal, and the roof features an ornamental dome, which is covered in cross-shaped tiles.

**Antiguo Palacio del
Arzobispado, Museo de la SHCP**
Calle Moneda 4,
Col. Centro, Cuauhtémoc
José Miguel de Rivera
15th century

011 A

1

Constructed in the early fifteenth century, this bright red building was the former Archbishopric Palace, until the nineteenth century when it began serving as the SHCP Art Museum. It displays a wide collection of Mexican art, by artists ranging from the eighteenth to twentieth centuries. The building's façade is crowned with inverted arches and decorative parapets. The interior has two glass dome-covered courtyards, lined with columned walkways on both levels, and the main staircase displays a large mural by José Gordillo.

Biblioteca de México · 012 A

Tolsa 4,
Col. Centro, Cuauhtémoc
Miguel Constanzó,
Antonio González Velázquez,
Ignacio de Castera, Abraham Zabludovsky
1807, 1987

The Biblioteca de México was originally built for a Tobacco Company in 1807. Shortly after, it was modified to serve as a prison. The building was declared a historical monument in 1931 and was transformed in a library in 1944, intended to hold the Mexican General Archives. It was named after José Vasconcelos, who was the director of the National Library at the time. In 1987, the Secretary of Education had the building remodelled by the architect Abraham Zabludovsky.

Restorations consisted of a 28,000 m² rectangular floor plan, with 4 × 1,600 m² interior courtyards, flooded with natural daylight. Abraham Zabludovsky's original design was supposed to acommodate 40,000 volumes. However, it turns out that the library can hold up to 250,000 pieces (such as books, magazines, newspapers). This public edifice has two main entrances on either side of the building, linked by an arcade, that accesses the courtyards. Columns and covered walkways line these spaces, providing access to all the adjoining rooms, which are distributed around these courtyards. One of the four courtyard spaces is semi-enclosed, containing a raised roof with an open void around its perimeter, still allowing adequate ventilation and sunlight to enter the space.

El Palacio de Hierro Centro
Av. 20 de Noviembre 3,
Col. Centro, Cuauhtémoc
J. Tron y Cía.
1888

El Palacio de Hierro Centro (Iron Palace) opened its doors in 1888, and was Mexico City's first department store (and the first of the retail chain). It was inspired by similar buildings of the period in Paris, London, New York, and Chicago. The department store's interior was severly damaged during a fire in 1914, but the Palacio de Hierro did not reopen its doors again until 1921, after a seven-year renovation period. The façade of this edifice has been unaltered until this day. The building's structure is made of iron and steel, and is cladded in concrete. The Tiffany stained glass windows are decoratively framed as is the dome.

Palacio de Bellas Artes

`014` `A`

Av. Juárez and
Eje Central Lázaro Cárdenas,
Col. Centro, Cuauhtémoc
Adamo Boari, Federico Mariscal
1904, 1934

The Palace of Fine Arts, situated on the Alameda Plaza, was declared a UNESCO monument in 1987. Initially designed by the Italian architect Adam Boari, the interior was later completed by the Mexican architect Federico Mariscal in 1934.

The exterior combines Art Nouveau and neoclassical styles. The Art Deco interior consists of marble, iron, and glass. Sculptures by Leonardo Bistolfi are displayed and a central roof, made of crystal, illuminates the interior. The lower level is dedicated to artworks and permanent murals and the level above is occupied by the National Architecture Museum exhibiting models, drawings, and photography of Mexican architects. The interior also houses a large theatre, home to the National Symphony Orchestra.

Gran Hotel Ciudad de México `015` `A`
Av. 16 de Septiembre 82,
Col. Centro, Cuauhtémoc
Unknown
1899

Situated at the heart of the city, the Grand Hotel offers views over the highly visited Zócalo and is recognised as one of Mexico City's most luxurious hotels. Constructed in 1899, it accomodated one of the first department stores in Mexico City. Its decorative Art Nouveau elements consist of exposed caged iron elevators, which run up to the colourful stained glass ceiling, which spreads over the entire hotel lobby space. Designed by renowned French artisan, Jacques Gruber, this highly ornate structure is one of the hotel's many breathtaking features. The lobby's atrium is surrounded by hallways lined with iron railings and columns, which merge into the ceiling's metal structure, acting as a support mechanism to the three domes that sit in the centre. With its wallpaper and predominantly carpeted floors, its interior's decor is remisnicent of another era.

Palacio de Correos   016 A

Calle Tacuba 1,
Col. Centro, Cuauhtémoc
Adamo Boari
1907

The Palacio de Correos (Postal Palace) was designed by the italian architect Adamo Boari, with a mix of gothic, baroque, art nouveau, and italian renaissance design principles. It has operated as a post office since 1907. The interior includes marble, steel, and copper materials with large skylit spaces and two divided staircases, which merge into one. The façade is made of chuluca (a light stone) and metal, and repetitive arches frame large windows. Its steel structure is earthquake resistant.

El Ángel de la Independencia, 017 A
Monumento a la Independencia «
Paseo de la Reforma,
Col. Juárez, Cuauhtémoc
Antonio Rivas Mercado
1910

The Monument of Independence (more commonly known as the Ángel de la Independencia) sits at the centre of a busy roundabout on the Paseo de la Reforma. It was designed by Antonio Rivas Mercado and completed in 1910 to pay tribute to the beginning of the War of Independence. The steel structure is cladded in stone, houses a tall, winding staircase, and reaches 36 m high. A gold coated statue of the Greek goddess of Victory crowns the top as a symbol of freedom. Similarly, its quadratic-shaped base is decorated with bronze and marble sculptures, which represent war, justice, and peace.

Iglesia de Nuestra Señora 018 A
de Guadalupe (del Buen Tono) ⩔
Plazuela de San Juan 15,
Col. Centro, Cuauhtémoc
Miguel Ángel de Quevedo
1912

The Iglesia de Nuestra Señora de Guadalupe (del Buen Tono) – the Church of Our Lady Guadalupe (the Church of Good Tone) – was built in 1875. Its site was formerly occupied by an ancient temple, which accomodated nuns and was later sold to a tobacco company who turned it into a theatre hall. The former temple was then demolished in 1911 and the current day church was completed in 1912. It was designed by the engineer Miguel Ángel de Quevedo with french influences, inclusive of the stained glass windows and lanterns. The arched ceiling inside the churches contain stained glass skylights, framed with sculptural elements.

1

View of Paseo de la Reforma, with the Monument of Independence at its centre

1

Edificio Basurto
Av. México 187,
Col. Condesa, Cuauhtémoc
Francisco José Serrano
1945

019 A

The Basurto building is another classic example of Art Deco style. The architect, Francisco José Serrano focused on the functional solution of spaces when designing this residential building. The combination of straight lines and curves develop a relationship between the interior spaces in terms of view, lighting, and ventilation. The orientation and geometric form of the reinforced concrete building allows sunlight to enter all four apartments on each of the fourteen levels. The central spiral staircase is a very characteristic element of the building.

Edificio Guardiola ⌄ 　020 A
Av. 5 de Mayo 707,
Col. Centro, Cuauhtémoc
Carlos Obregón Santacilia
1928

The Guardiola building comprises nine levels, three of which are basements. Its large volumetric form is crowned by a body of two retracted levels. The building's appearance reflects on Art Deco styles, and the interior is structured around two perpendicular axes, which define the internal circulation. Elevators at the intersection of these axes shape the central space.

Edificio La Nacional ⌄ 　022 A
Av. Juárez 4,
Col. Centro, Cuauhtémoc
Manuel Ortiz Monasterio
1932

The Art Deco style office building was designed by Manuel Ortiz Monasterio and sits directly across the famous Palacio de Bellas Artes in the city centre. With a height of 55 m it was initially one of Mexico City's tallest buildings. The 15,000 m² building has a total of 13 floors, and its steel structure is cladded in reinforced concrete in order to withstand earthquakes.

Hotel Fiesta Americana » 　021 A
Paseo de la Reforma 80,
Col. Juárez, Cuauhtémoc
Héctor Mestre, Manuel de la Colina
1970

The Fiesta Americana Hotel is a five star hotel opened in 1970. The 25-floor hotel was designed by the architects Héctor Mestre and Manuel de la Colina. This L-shaped building reaches a height of 96 m, and is made of glass and concrete. It is composed of three parts: a two-floor base, which serves the main lobby, bars, and conference rooms; the main element, which accomodates 622 people over 20 floors, has flat and ridged façades, covered with a myriad of windows. Crowning the top of the hotel is the third element in which are set a restaurant and a gym.

**Iglesia de la Santa Cruz
y la Soledad** ⩘
Plaza de La Soledad,
Venustiano Carranza
Cayetano de Sigüenza,
Ignacio de Castera,
Ildefonso Iniesta Bejarano,
Francisco Antonio de Guerrero y Torres
1750, 1787, 1982

023 A

The Roman Parish Iglesia de la Soledad was originally designed with Augustinian principles and later rebuilt with neo-classical influences. The interior elements consist of a marble altar, which was built in 1903 along with the pulpit and the balustrade of the choir. It was declared a national monument in 1931 and was restored again in 1982.

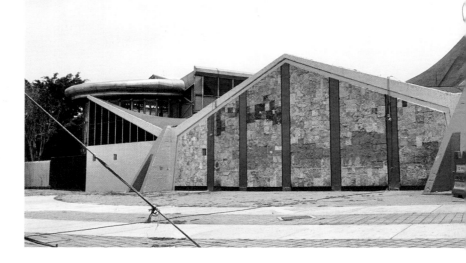

Iglesia de la Inmaculada Concepción ⌂ »
Belisario Domínguez 7,
Centro Histórico
Unknown
16th century

The Church of Immaculate Conception was founded in the sixteenth century and was originally the first cloister for nuns. With the baroque influences of the interior vaults and the dome, this building also draws upon neoclassical styles, recognisable in its decorative white elements and tower, which was never completed.

Estación San Lázaro « 025 A
Av. Eduardo Molina
and Calz. Gral. Ignacio Zaragoza,
Col. 7 de Julio y 10 de Mayo,
Venustiano Carranza
Félix Candela
1969

The San Lázaro metro station was designed by the Spanish architect Félix Candela. Structurally, its roof consists of a series of hyperbolic paraboloids, which is typical in Candela's architecture. Glass windows link the edges of the complex structure allowing daylight to enter the interior spaces. Its fine series of concrete canopies form the coverage for naturally illuminated circulation spaces.

Torre Latinoamericana　026 A
Eje Central Lázaro Cárdenas 2,
Col. Centro, Cuauhtémoc
Augusto H. Álvarez,
Alfonso González Paullada
1956

The Torre Latinoamericana was designed by the Mexican modernist architects, Augusto H. Álvarez and Alfonso González Paullada. It was the world's first tallest building to have been constructed with glass and aluminium, as well as the first skyscraper to be built within a highly active seismic zone. The skyscraper's construction began in 1948 and was completed in 1956, at which time it was the largest building in Latin America. Located in Mexico City's busy centre, on the corner of Madero Street and Eje Central, with a height of 204 m (if you include the antenna at its top), the Torre Latinoamericana remained Mexico City's tallest skyscraper until 1972. The steel structure was truely recognised for its structural design after withstanding the earthquakes of 1957, 1985, and 2012. This 28,000 m² building has 44 levels above ground and three basement levels. A public observation deck on the fourty-fourth level provides a panoramic view over Mexico City's historic centre.

1

Monumento a la Revolución   027 A
Plaza de la República s/n,
Col. Tabacalera, Cuauhtémoc
Émile Bénard,
Carlos Obregón Santacilia
1938

This landmark monument commemorates the Mexican Revolution, hence its name: Monument to the Revolution. It is 67 m tall. A design competition for the monument was held in 1897, which was won by the French architect Émile Bénard. It was originally designed to be the Federal Legislative Palace, with neoclassical characteristics. However, due to the violence during the Mexican Revolution and lack of funding, the construction was put on hold in 1912. It was completed in 1938 with an Art Deco design by Carlos Obregón Santacilia. The shape of the monument rises from its quadrical base with four columns of sculpted arches, which support the double dome crown. An elevator, and stairways, lie inside the columns and lead up to the terrace above, which provides panoramic views from the 26 m high structure. 8 m high voids sit between the ambulatory and viewing area, allowing light into the interior of the dome. Its façade consists of Italian marble, and Norwegian granite.

027 A

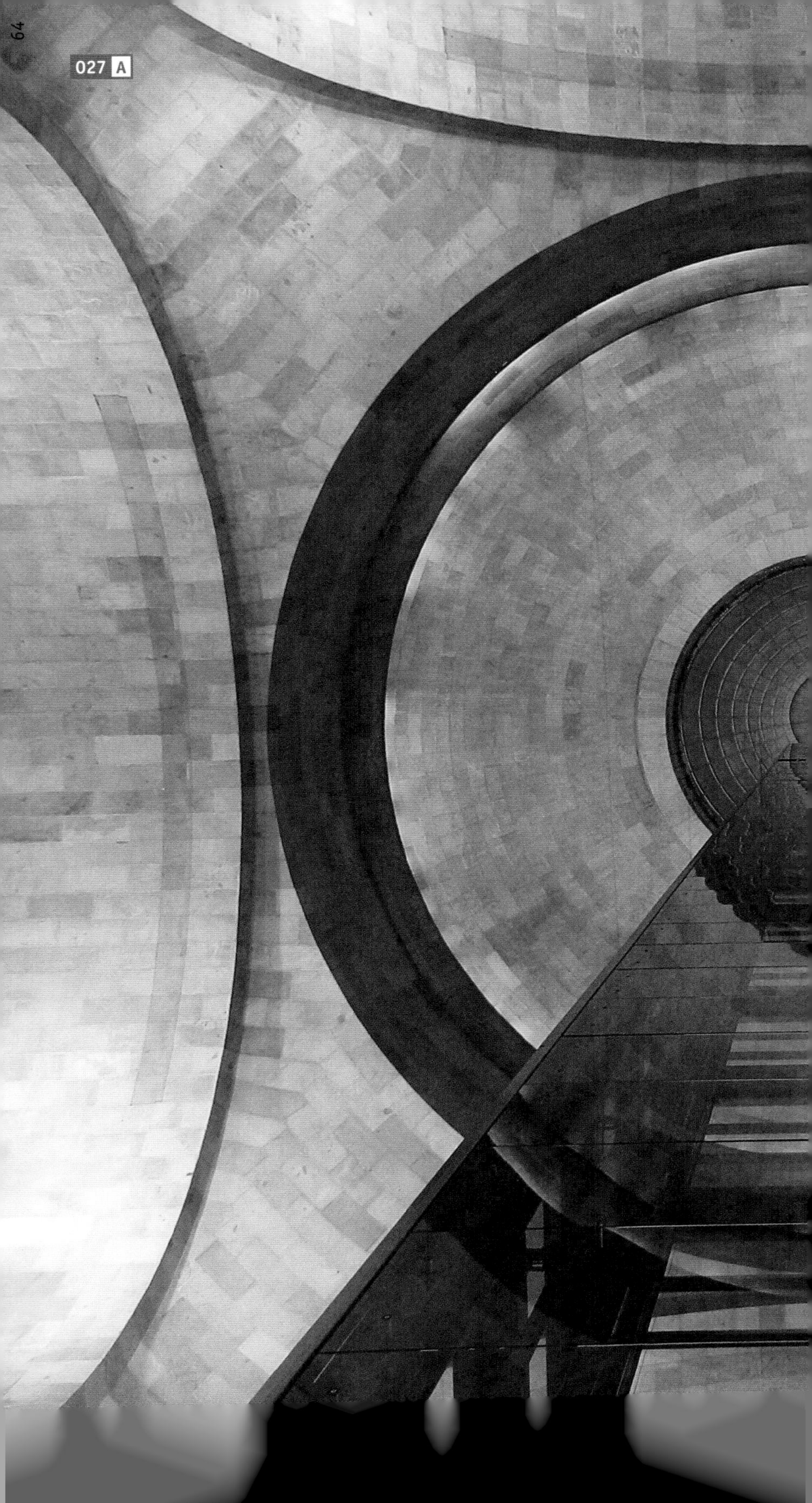

1

Plaza de las Tres Culturas
Eje Central Lázaro Cárdenas
and Av. Ricardo Flores Magón,
Nonoalco Tlatelcoco, Cuauhtémoc
Mario Pani
1966

028 A

The Three Cultures Square can be found in the Tlatelolco neighbourhood. It was designed by the Mexican architect and urbanist, Mario Pani, and completed in 1966. The plaza comprises a large main square, surrounded by buildings, which are representative of the three following eras of Mexican History: the Pre Hispanic, the Spanish Colonial, and the Modern. The ruins and pyramids of an Aztec temple are obviously part of the Pre-Hispanic era. The Spanish Colonial culture is represented by the Santiago de Tlatelolco catholic church, which was built during the sixteenth century. The culture of modern Mexico is expressed by the Conjunto Urbano Nonoalco Tlatelolco (the largest residential housing complex of Mexico), and the Tower of Tlatelolco, which used to house the Mexican Ministry of Foreign Affairs main headquarters. Today, this building is used for the University Cultural Center. The Plaza de las Tres Culturas also contains two memorial monuments, in commemoration of the victims of both the 1521 and 1968 Tlatelolco massacres.

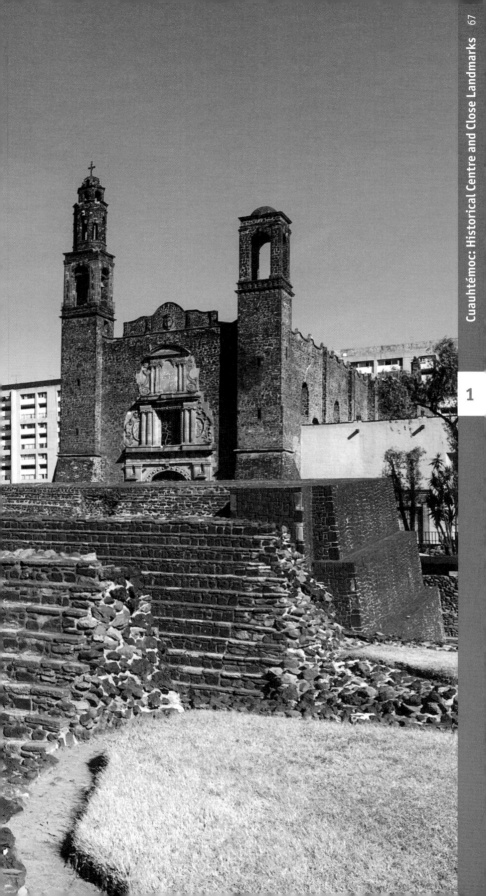

Estación de Bomberos
Ave Fénix «   029 A
Av. Fénix
Insurgentes Centro, Col. San Rafael
AT103, BGP Arquitectura
2007

From the outside, this 2,400 m² firestation looks like a simple elevated aluminium box, set within a normal streetscape. The architects designed the building's interior in such a way that intertwines public and private spaces, and incorporates training and information programs for the general public. These public and private spaces have been organised over four levels. These circular voids have also been cut into the roof and ceilings, serving as lightwells and skylights. Perforations that vary in diameter, connect the different levels, generating vertical and horizontal flow of light and movement. The first storey's 7 m height serves as a covered patio, open to the street.

Reforma 222 ⍢   030 A
Paseo de la Reforma 222,
Col. Juárez, Cuauhtémoc
Teodoro González de León
2007

Designed by the Mexican architect Teodoro González de León and completed in 2007, this complex consists of three separate towers. Two of them are the tallest on the Paseo de la Reforma – 126 m high – with respectively 31 and 26 floors. The third tower is 94 m high – with only 19 floors. All three towers are made of a mixture of glass, steel and reinforced concrete, and are used for residential, commercial, and office spaces. The façades' structure consists of a double glazed envelope with 4.10 m high and 1.60 m wide panels. The first layer of these window panes are of extra clear glass, and the second of tempered glass, which controls ultraviolet rays, saves energy and reduces acoustics.

1

BMV (Stock Exchange) « `031 A`
Paseo de la Reforma 255,
Col. Cuauhtémoc, Cuauhtémoc
Juan José Díaz Infante
1999

The BMV building is the only stock exchange office in Mexico City and is located in the financial district. Designed by Juan José Díaz Infante, it was opened in 1999. The building's skin consists of glazed panels in shades of black and blue. The modernist building entails two separate bodies; a dome structure and a tower with three slim entities that are adjoined and cut at different angles – the central body reaching the heighest.

Centro Telefónico San Juan ⩢ `032 A`
Ernesto Pugibet and Buen Tono,
Col. Centro, Cuauhtémoc
Héctor Mestre, Manuel de la Colina
1969

The San Juan call-centre belongs to the telecommunications company, Telmex. It was designed by architects Héctor Mestre and Manuel de la Colina and completed in 1969. The building form embodies a 100 m high tower, and a set of adjoining buildings. Three of the tower's platforms hold antenna microwave systems of high, medium and low capacity. The concrete structure was greatly damaged by the 1985 earthquake.

Cuauhtémoc: Historical Centre and Close Landmarks

1

Conjunto Veracruz
Av. Veracruz 79–91,
Col. Condesa, Cuauhtémoc
JSᵃ
2002

Located on Veracruz Avenue in the Condesa neighbourhood, this group of five buildings are closely related to one another and to the surrounding context. A series of open spaces and connecting landscapes sit within the interior of the block. Veracruz I (no. 79) is the first building of the group and is located at the intersection of three streets. The project is resolved by means of a curved section of exposed concrete that accentuates the outline of the street. The interiors of the three single-floor apartments and the double-height duplex penthouse are reflected through the façade. Veracruz II (no. 81) is the second building on Veracruz, which neighbours the first construction. It is located on an irregular L-shaped lot with 8 m of frontage. The design continues to the interior patio of the first building and matches it in height. It is composed of two volumes, for which the domestic spaces are distributed in the frontal, while the exterior serves as an independent studio-workshop for each apartment.

Glazed footbridges and an external stairway connect the two volumes. Veracruz III (no. 85 to no. 91) is the third project of the series and consists of an adaption from an old tenement house. The façade along Veracruz and the first bay of the volume were salvaged to create four small two-level houses, with direct access from the street. A new, lighter structure was integrated atop the original volume, with two apartments set back from the façade to create a terrace. At the back of the lot, a new building rises with ten apartments: five duplexes on the ground floor and first level, each with their own private patio, and above them five triplexes with private terraces. The development is completed by a seven-storey building at the far end. This building consists of two blocks of dwellings, one facing the street and the other the interior patio. Veracruz V (no. 83) is the last of the series and is erected on a lot situated between the second and third projects, on the same scale as these two. The volume contains three apartments and a multi-purpose space on the ground floor. The first two apartments serve as independent dwellings, whereas the third apartment is a three-level penthouse contained in a recessed volume that opens onto a terrace overlooking the avenue.

Tlaxcala 190 «   034 A

Tlaxcala 190,
Col. Condesa, Cuauhtémoc
Rojkind Arquitectos
2003

Designed by Rojkind Arquitectos, the Tlaxcala apartment building is situated in the Condensa neighbourhood. Each floor consists of 4×90 m² apartments and 4×165 m² double height penthouses. The façade is made of transparent glass, interrupted by railed balconies and operable panels with stainless steel frames and flexible tubes of translucent, multicolored plastic. The core of the complex is hollowed-out by an elliptic-shaped central lobby, which rises to the top of the building. Glazed bridges connect the vertical circulation on either side. A latticework of white pre-poured concrete covers the skin of the lobby linking all of the floor levels.

Torre Mayor ⌄   035 A

Paseo de la Reforma 505
Col. Cuauhtémoc, Cuauhtémoc
Zeidler Partnership Architects,
Adamson Associates Architects
2003

The Torre Mayor is one of Mexico City's tallest structures – 225 m high. It was completed in 2003 and designed by the Canadian Zeidler Partnership Architects and Adamson Associates Architects. The building's contemporary form comprises a quadrical volume, which is connected to a curved sail-like volume. Its façade is made of reinforced structural bracing to ensure it withstands earthquakes. The curved southern façade is completely glazed and provides thermal and acoustic isolation. The northern façade consists of precast granite. All 55 floors of the building are column free, and all services are enclosed in its central core.

1

Centro Cultural Vladimir Kaspé 036 A

Universidad La Salle,
Av. Benjamín Franklin 47,
Col. Condesa, Cuauhtémoc
Gerardo Broissin Covarrubias,
Gabriel Covarrubias González,
Jorge Hernández de la Garza
2006

The Vladimir Kaspé Cultural Centre is situated within the University campus of La Salle University. It was designed by Broissin Architects and completed in 2006. The building's solid concrete façade consists of metal columns and thickened glass, which define the access to the centre. An exterior ramp gives the users access to the vast open spaces of all levels. The ramp ends on the last level, where, by passing through a glass box one is lead into a singular space intended for exhibitons. The large glased surface allows natural light to fill the spaces.

Biblioteca Vasconcelos 037 A

Eje 1 Norte Mosqueta
and Juan Aldama,
Col. Buenavista, Cuauhtémoc
*Alberto Kalach, Gustavo Lipkau,
Juan Palomar, Tonatiuh Martínez*
2006

This library was named after the philosopher, educator, and presidential candidate José Vasconcelos, and is a renowned example of modern architecture. The ceiling and the glass walls, create a naturally illuminated space, which plays with transparencies in all the levels of the library. Its concrete structure consists of hanging shelves made of steel and glass. The long foyer in the ground floor distributes users to the different rooms and spaces.

1

Centro Cultural España «≈   038 A

República de Guatemala 18,
Col. Centro, Cuauhtémoc
JSª
2010

Spain's Cultural Center was designed by JSª, with the intent to enhance and consolidate the interior spaces,in order to host a diversity of events and exhibits. The architects hoped that the cultural centre would be considered as a passageway, linking different zones and different cultural programs, sponsored by the Historic Center. The building's program envisages several floors with polyvalent uses that work as exhibit areas, conference rooms for seminars, workshops, childrens' activities, plays, concerts and other such cultural events. This building's structure provides large open spaces, without intermediate columns. The design also aims to integrate the building into its historic context in a contemporary manner. The façade and volume respect the proportions of the street and the surrounding buildings. The materials used for the façade consist of concrete and Corten steel, with lattices and recesses, that seek to imitate the colors and depth of the façades of the other downtown buildings.

Cholula ≋   039 A

Cholula 90,
Col. Condesa, Cuauhtémoc
Archetonic
2003

The four-level Cholula 90 apartment block was designed by Archetonic and completed in 2003. The building is made up of two separate bodies, which each contain six apartments. These are connected through a covered central stairwell. The buildings façade consists of horizontal and vertical elements of opalescent glass and concrete.

1

Museo Memoria y Tolerancia 040 A
Av. Juárez 8,
Col. Centro, Cuauhtémoc
Arditti + RDT Arquitectos
2010

The Museo Memoria y Tolerancia (Museum of Memory and Tolerance) was designed as an architectural space that coexists amongst all people. It integrates the commemoration of genocides provoked by racial discrimination (Memory) and the unforgiving legacy left behind, which must lead us to respect of others and coexistence in diversity (Tolerance). The Museum is constructed with reinforced concrete and steel over seven levels. The Museum focuses on sustaining the *floating* Children's Memorial, which is why the interior atrium – the volume that contains the Memory and Tolerance permanent exhibits – is displayed like two open arms embracing the Children's Memorial. On the interior atrium, the different functions of the building are seen as independent volumes. The Museum's permanent exhibits (Memory and Tolerance) are held behind the exposed concrete L-shaped mass. A wooden box holds the auditorium, which cantilevers over a ramp that leads towards the lower Children's Educational Area. At the same time, its top serves as a base to host the Temporary Exhibition Hall, which leads visitors through a recessed transparent enclosure. The administration is held behind a dark granite element, separated from the upper main exhibition area by a glazed gap that integrates an Educational Center, linked by a transparent ramped corridor to a Public Library within the colonnade overlooking the Juárez Plaza. Horizontal circulations are incorporated as superimposed balconies that provide views of the interior space.

Plaza Residences «» 041 A

Paseo de la Reforma 77,
Col. Tabacalera, Cuauhtémoc
Migdal Arquitectos
2010

Plaza Residences hotel is an emblematic building, flanked by two cultural landmarks that enroot it with the historic past of the area, the Monument to Columbus and the Monument to the Revolution. The shape of the building gives richness and movement to the urban context. In response to the Columbus traffic circle, the building, with its glass interior façade, is erected in the shape of a hook, creating a concave interior space. This concave shape opens up and embraces the majestic traffic circle, and allows each apartment to have a view on the avenue. The first floors accommodate common, commercial areas and services. Its principal façade looks like a smooth-skinned glass curtain. The building's skin is accentuated with randomly placed aluminum mullions, which control the effect of the sun, while creating an interesting effect of light and shadow in the concave shape. The rounded shape and horizontal bands of this convex façade, shape the building's hallways that run the entire length of the building, providing a unique view of Mexico City.

Lisboa 7 » 042 A

Calle Lisboa 7,
Col. Juárez, Cuauhtémoc
AT103
2010

The Lisboa 7 project is a residential apartment block, designed by the AT103 architecture firm, to become part of the existing social fabric. The maximum allowed density was divided into six volumes. Each volume is 3.60 m wide, and has a 4 m wide separation, allowing each space to receive cross ventilation and light. All living spaces face westwards; the east side is closed almost entirely, in order to provide privacy for each unit. The east façade of each volume is a vertical garden, which provides views from all units. The block comprises sixty modules of 36 m², which is the minimum required surface for housing in Mexico. A range of different modular units were incorporated, from 36 m² (1 module) to 144 m² (4 modules). The building has five levels and only two corridors, on the second and fourth floors, where the entrances to the first to third-storey units are located. Each module consists of a free floor plan and service area, with water supply for either a kitchen or a bathroom, and can be programmed to suit each user's preference. The materials employed for the project are basic construction materials with no further finishings, cinder block and exposed concrete for the structure.

Centro de Legalidad y Justicia   043 A
República de Brasil 74
and República de Paraguay 37,
Col. Centro, Cuauhtémoc
*JS*ª
2011

The Centro de Legalidad y Justicia (Legal and Justice Centre) consists of two buildings. The first – the Brasil building – is a three-level building with two green interior patios, built during the eighteenth and nineteenth centuries, whereas the second – the Paraguay building – was built during the nineteenth century. Both have been adapted to accomodate office spaces and agencies of the Federal District Government that operate in the historic centre, such as the Federal District Attorney General's Office. The Brasil unit also contains several multiple-use rooms, a kitchenette, and spaces for security and administration. Public areas are located on the ground floor and an open terrace is located on the roof.

Hotel Carlota ⩧ 044 A
Río Amazonas 73,
Col. Cuauhtémoc, Cuauhtémoc
JSª
2015

Amsterdam Tower » 045 A
Av. Insurgentes 301–303,
Col. Condesa, Cuauhtémoc
JSª
2011

The Hotel Carlota is a redevelopment of the former Hotel Jardín Amazonas. It was designed by JSª and completed in 2015. The building's typical structure was retained along with the stairs, exterior corridors, ceilings, balconies, and central courtyard that offers an oasis within the city. Today, the hotel has 36 rooms, each with their individual and unique style. The façade, which was remodeled with modernist qualities in the 1980s was left untouched although it was covered with a reflective layer of glazing. The concrete structure of the existing building can be appreciated from every common area and hotel room. Access through the façade was avoided by locating the buildings main entrance along the side of the neighbouring parking lot that leads directly into the central courtyard space, which is the busiest public space, surrounded by the restaurant. The shop/gallery, and library have integrated spaces with the courtyard. The interior consist of a lattice of black concrete blocks, and contemporary art covers some walls of the rooms, creating a very unique spacial experience.

JSª connected six adjacent plots with development potential, and designed an urban complex of mixed uses: public parking, shops, offices, and housing. New buildings were added to the existing, in the form of housing projects facing the residential area of the Colonia Condesa, and commercial projects facing Insurgentes Avenue. The residential apartments face the Condesa neighbourhood, ensuring that access to the apartments is always done through the residential neighbourhood, while access to the other programs is done through Insurgentes Avenue. The Amsterdam tower forms part of the mixed-use complex, formed by two buildings facing towards Amsterdam Street and two buildings facing towards Insurgentes Avenue, with a common plaza in the middle. It is one of the highest tower on the avenue with a total of nineteen levels, offering public parking on the first six levels and apartments from the seventh onwards. The apartments were designed taking maximum advantage of the orientation, with views to the south and to the Condesa neighbourhood.

Torre BBVA Bancomer

046 A

Paseo de la Reforma 510,
Col. Juárez, Cuauhtémoc
Legorretta+Legorretta,
Rogers Stirk Harbour + Partners
2012

Torre BBVA Bancomer is a 50-storey office building with a first level of triple height. Glass elevators lift you from the ground floor to the sky lobby on the twelfth floor. A terrace is located on the roof, providing views over the Chapultepec Park, as well a serving as an exhibition and public event space. The façade structure is made of steel bracing. The geometry of the diagonal structure establishes a lattice frame, providing protection from the light and heat of the sun.

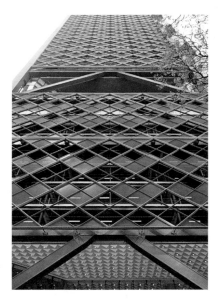

Krystal Grand Reforma Uno »   047 A
Paseo de la Reforma 1,
Col. Tabacalera, Cuauhtémoc
Unknown
1995

Located in the centre of Mexico City, the awarded Krystal Grand Reforma Uno is a luxurious upscale hotel. The building's skin consists of concrete and glazed panels. The hotel itself features a 20-storey atrium lobby, decorated with monumental abstract sculptures, and furnished with brass-ribbed gazebo seating areas. All 489 rooms are spacious, and offer modern first class amenities. This hotel also hosts an exclusive spa with six massage rooms, an indoor pool, three hot tubs and a sauna.

Reforma 27 ≈   048 A
Paseo de la Reforma 27,
Col. Tabacalera, Cuauhtémoc
Taller de Arquitectura X, Alberto Kalach
2012

Reforma 27 is a residential building, whose interior comprises of open floor plans, which enable the distribution of different modular apartments, which vary from 40 m² to 240 m². The shape of the building consists of two volumes, separated from one another with an open courtyard. The profile of this residential tower is in the shape of an H. The building's skin is made of red reinforced concrete and glass, which make up the shelf like façade wall.

Havre 69 ReUrbano « ⌃   `049` `A`
Havre 69,
Col. Juárez, Cuauhtémoc
AT103
2013

Mercado Roma ⌄   `050` `A`
Querétaro 225,
Col. Roma Norte, Cuauhtémoc
Rojkind Arquitectos, Cadena + Asociados
2014

1

Havre 69 ReUrbano is located on the southern end of Paseo de la Reforma. Its street-front shell is a nineteenth century structure, which originally accommodated four upper-middle-class homes. The architecture firm, AT103, divided these houses into twelve housing units, offices, two commercial front stores, a bakery, and a low-cost prefix menu establishment. The narrow, corridor-like plazas, on either side of the building, open the space around this building, connecting it directly with the neighbourhood by providing free access to the existing building's composition.

The Roma Market was designed by Rojkind Arquitectos and Cadena + Asociados Concept Design, to favour encounters and interactions. The market seeks to integrate local efforts and launch them from a contemporary platform. An industrial space, formerly occupied by the well known Bar León, was repurposed for this project. There are fifty-three vending stalls on the street level, which reinterpret the traditional market grid. The two upper mezzanine levels house various restaurants and a food court, a terrace and an open air space with a fully functional vertical vegetable garden.

Important landmarks around Cuauhtémoc

The districts of Gustavo A. Madero, Iztacalco, and Venustiano Carranza are located in the northern part of Mexico City. The Gustavo A. Madero district is home to one of the city's most famous tourist attractions: the Basílica de Santa María de Guadalupe, which is on the Plaza de las Américas and attracts thousands of tourists annually. The Iztacalco district is the smallest and is situated northeast of the city centre, bordering the Benito Juárez and Iztapalapa districts. It is predominantly a residential, industrial, and commercial area, and is home to Mexico City's Palace of Sports. The Venustiano Carranza district is also situated in the northeast and is an extension of Cuauhtémoc, the historic city centre. It is a cultural and recreational zone, home to a majority of the city's traditional markets, particularly the Mercado de la Merced.

Basílica de Santa María de
Guadalupe (original and new)
Plaza de las Américas 1,
Col. Villa de Guadalupe,
Gustavo A. Madero
Pedro de Arrieta, Pedro Ramírez Vázquez,
Gabriel Chávez de la Mora
1709, 1976

The old and new Basílicas de Santa María de Guadalupe are situated on the Plaza de las Américas. The original Roman Catholic basilica was built in 1709. Its interior was severely damaged after a bomb exploded in 1921. Due to its unstable foundations, the new modern-style basilica built in 1976, which houses the original image of Our Lady of Guadalupe. Its circular floor plan is 100 m in diameter and provides a view of the Virgin anywhere from inside the edifice. This basilica can welcome 10,000 people. There are a total of twenty-one chapels on all three levels of the basilica. Its seven doors were designed to represent the seven gates of Celestial Jerusalem.

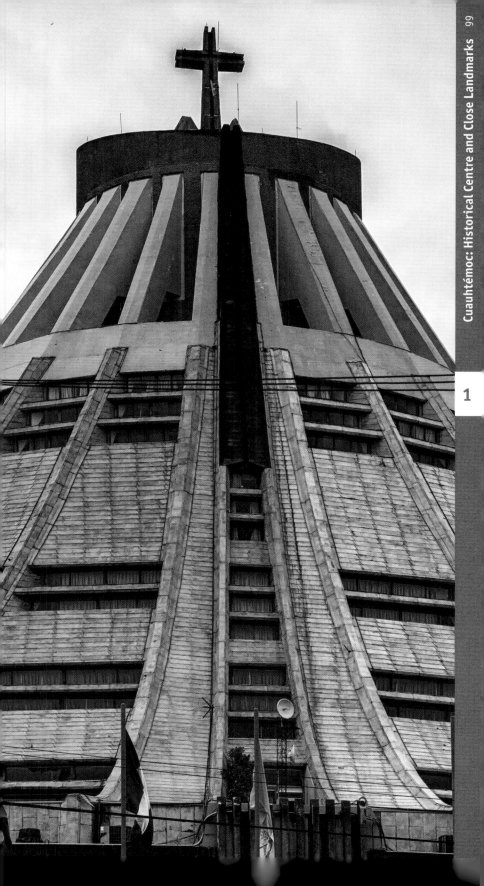

Palacio de los Deportes

052 A

Av. Viaducto Río de la Piedad
and Río Churubusco,
Col. Granjas México, Iztacalco
Félix Candela, Antonio Peyri,
Enrique Castañeda Tamborell
1968

The Palace of Sports, designed by the architects Félix Candela, Antonio Peyri, and Enrique Castañeda Tamborell was completed in 1968, in time for the Olympic Games of that same year. With a seating capacity of up to 26,000, it hosts concerts, trade fairs, exhibitions and sporting events. The indoor area contains four bleachers, corporate offices, and facilities for food, beverage, and health services. Its spherical floor plan is also expressed in its dome form that is made up of an arched structural web of aluminum tubes, which supports the hyperbolic paraboloid sheets of copper. Secondary supporting systems include V-shaped concrete columns that line the entrance accessways.

1

Planetario Luis Enrique Erro 053 A
Av. Wilfrido Massieu s/n,
Col. San Pedro Zacatenco,
Gustavo A. Madero
Víctor Alcérreca,
Territorios Taller de Arquitectura,
Hesner Sánchez, Fermín Andrade
1967, 2007

The Luis Enrique Erro Planetarium was originally completed in 1967 and later remodelled in 2007 to modernise its technological systems. It is Mexico's first planetarium and one of the largest in Latin America. This planetarium is part of the National Polytechnic Institute and is a Center for Dissemination of Science and Technology. The building's symbolic façade entrance is made of glass pannels and features a concrete dome, which covers a large portion of the roof. The open roof area surrounding the dome acts as a platform for stargazing and provides panoramic views over the city.

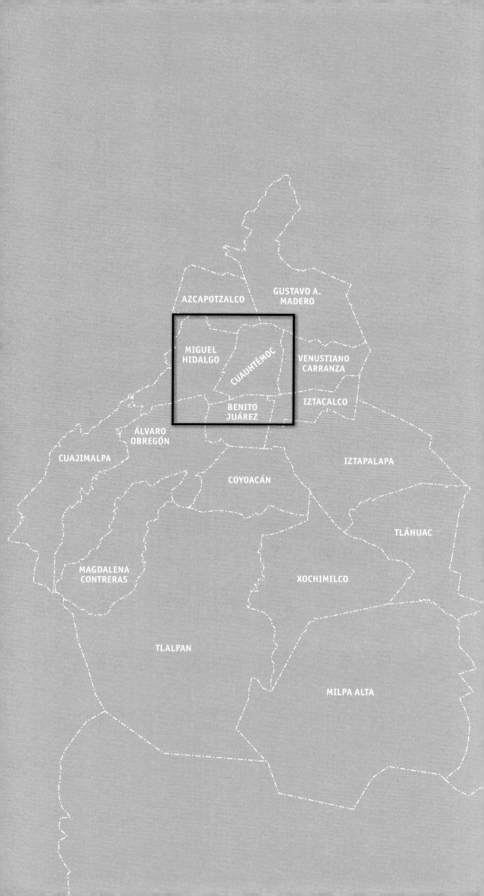

West of Cuauhtémoc: Commercial and Diplomatic Districts

West of Cuauhtémoc: Commercial and Diplomatic Districts

The Miguel Hidalgo district is located in the northwest of Mexico City at the border of the State of Mexico. It is named after Miguel Hidalgo y Costilla who lead the Mexican War of Independence in the early eighteenth century. In terms of the quantity of daily visitors, it comes second after the Cuauhtémoc district. This district has a large amount of vegetation and green space – one of its largest parks being the Chapultepec Park. This hilly upper-class district is mostly residential and commercial, but also contains some of Mexico City's most renowned attractions, such as the contemporary Soumaya Museum, the National Museum of Anthropology and the National Auditorium. Many five star hotels and restaurants are located in this area. Some of the most popular neighbourhoods of this district are Polanco, Granada, Tacuba, Tacubaya, and Lomas de Chapultepec.

Castillo de Chapultepec 054 A
Bosque de Chapultepec,
Col. Bosque de Chapultepec,
Miguel Hidalgo
Julius Hofmann, Carl Gangolf Kayser,
Carlos Schaffer, Eleuterio Méndez,
Ramón Rodríguez Arangoiti
17th and 18th centuries

The Castillo de Chapultepec was built during the seventeenth century on a rock formation at the centre of the Chapultepec Park, originally a sacred place for the Aztecs. This castle has taken on many uses, but serves today as the National History Museum. The European and Mexican architects, Julius Hofmann, Carlos Schaffer, Carl Gangolf Kaiser, Ramón Rodríguez Arangoiti and Eleuterio Méndez played a part in the renovations of the nowadays neo-classical style castle. The castle includes a tower, monument and a large roof top garden, which provides panoramic views over the Miguel Hidalgo district. Its interior features decorative timber, marble and stained glass windows. Skylights also illuminate the mezzanine spaces.

054 A

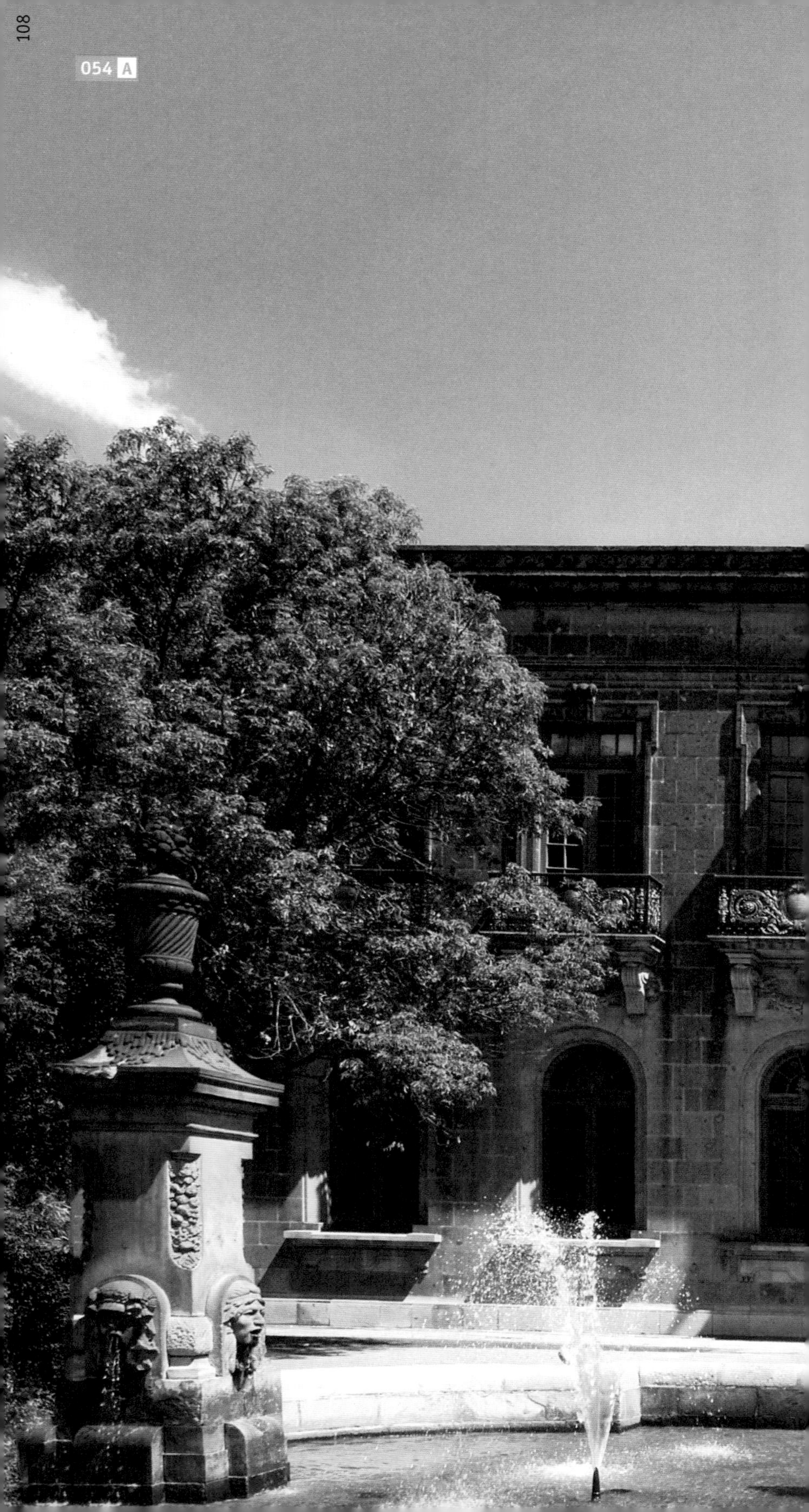

2

Benemérita Escuela
Nacional de Maestros
Calzada México-Tacuba 75,
Col. Un Hogar para nosotros,
Miguel Hidalgo
Mario Pani
1925, 1947

055 A

The Benemérita Escuela Nacional de Maestros is an educational institution for preschool, primary, and secondary students. It was designed by the Mexican architect, Mario Pani. The school's design is based on geometric forms. The red and white envelope is composed of long, thin, horizontal strips, made of red brick, interspersed with various openings, framed in white. Tall white columns mark the sheltered walkways that access the classrooms. A large mural, by José Clemente Orozco, is featured at one end of the open air auditorium space.

Edificio Ermita » ↲
Av. Revolución 23,
Col. Tacubaya, Miguel Hidalgo
Juan Segura Gutiérrez
1930

The Ermita building was designed by the renowned Mexican architect, Juan Segura Gutiérrez, and completed in 1930. It is one of Mexico City's most influential buildings of the first half of the twentieth century, and is a reference for the spanish republican exile, since a great number of Spanish families, living in exile in Mexico, came to live in the Ermita building. This edifice is also known as the Triangle of Tacubaya, since it sits at one of the most important street crossings of the city. Its triangular floor plate is designed around an open courtyard. It has nine storeys and is 35 m high. Its first six levels are mainly reserved for commercial and retail spaces, as well as a large cinema, which is located on the first floor, known as the Cine Hipódromo Condesa. The residential spaces, of various dimensions, are mainly located on the last three levels. Spread arches provide access into the building and underline the art deco styles of the facades.

El Palacio de Hierro Polanco « 057 A
Av. Moliere 222,
Col. Polanco, Miguel Hidalgo
Ignacio de la Hidalga (1891),
Paul Dubois (1920)
1891, 1920

This building of 55,200 m², houses one of the Palacio de Hierro (Iron Palace) department stores, in the upper class neighbourhood of Polanco. It reopened in 2016, after an extensive renovation and expansion. It is now the largest department store in Latin America. The original building was designed by the architect Ignacio de la Hidalga, but was destroyed by a fire. The current building was designed by the french architect, Paul Dubois and completed in 1920. It is made up of various geometric shapes, such as cuboids, triangular prisms, and a cylinder, which have been merged to create one entity. Square voids, set on a grid, serve as the façade's windows.

**Parroquia de San Antonio
de las Huertas**
058 A
Calzada México-Tacuba 70,
Col. Tlaxpana, Miguel Hidalgo
*Félix Candela, Enrique De la Mora,
Fernando López Carmona*
1956

The San Antonio de las Huertas Parish was designed by the Spanish-Mexican architect Félix Candela in 1956. The parish was built on land, which belonged to the franciscan convent of San Antonio de las Huertas, until the nineteenth century. Despite its avant-garde design and hyperbolic paraboloid structure, it remains unknown today. The arched concrete roof of the church is comprised of three large vaults, that are aligned and spaced from one another, encasing the nave. The stained glass windows that follow these vaults illuminate the interior of the church in amber hues.

Iglesia de San Ignacio de Loyola
Av. Horacio and Moliere,
Col. Polanco, Miguel Hidalgo
Juan Sordo Madaleno
1962

The San Ignacio Church was designed by the Mexican architect Juan Sordo Madaleno, and was completed in 1962. Its triangular theme delivers a sturdy structure, all the while creating a unique form, which stongly emphasises verticality. The church's façade is predominantly constructed of brick, timber, and black steel, which is arranged in the form of a grid, serving as a frame for the exterior and interior walls, enclosing the concrete walls. The black steel is used as trussed drafters for the roof support, these simultaneously serving as a place to hang the church's light fixtures. The large stained glass windows at the end of the nave, above the entrance, and on either side of the transept, produce a multi-coloured atmosphere within. A large cross is fixed behind the narrow, white altar. Simple wooden benches line the nave, creating a wide central isle. The flooring of the church is polished grey stone.

Museo Nacional de Antropología
Paseo de la Reforma and Calzada Gandhi,
Col. Bosque de Chapultepec,
Miguel Hidalgo
Pedro Ramírez Vázquez, Jorge Campuzano,
Rafael Mijares Alcérreca
1964

The National Museum of Anthropology is a contemporary museum, designed by Pedro Ramírez Vázquez, Rafael Mijares Alcérreca, and Jorge Campuzano. Located in the Chapultepec park, it is one of the most visited museums in Latin America, with up to 2 million visitors per year. The construction of this 80,000 m² edifice was completed in 1964. A little more than half of the building's surface is dedicated to the twenty-three permanent exhibition rooms, which feature archaeological and anthropological artifacts from the Mexican pre-Columbian heritage, as well as reconstructions of Mayan temples. Many of these exhibition spaces lead to the outdoor gardens (also exhibiton areas). The National Museum of Anthropology also has a large open air courtyard at its centre. At the centre of this courtyard: a pond, adorned with lush aquatic plants. A singular pillar supporting a massive concrete slab, called the *umbrella,* shelters a large portion of the outdoor area.

Edificio Temp ≋»
Anatole France 31
Col. Polanco, Miguel Hidalgo
Archetonic
2004

061 A

The Temp building is located in the upper-class neighbourhood of Polanco. Its four bodies are separated by courtyards and bridges, and are naturally lit through their translucent façades. Two axes in a cross formation emerge from these bodies; the one closer to the street provides access to each block of lofts; the other is used as a garden with palm trees, which filter the view between the rear and front blocks to create a tree-filled oasis.

Torre Reforma 115 »
Paseo de la Reforma 115,
Col. Lomas de Chapultepec,
Miguel Hidalgo
Arquitectos Brom Asociados
2005

062 A

The Torre Reforma 115 is a 120 m skyscraper that culminates at a total of 27 levels, with a helicopter landing pad on the roof. Its façade consists of a double glazed envelope, which is made of an energy saving, tempered glass. Large chunks seem to have been removed from the east edge of the building's solid geometric shape, leaving one singular column to support the terraces and the immense, partially covered entrance plaza that remain.

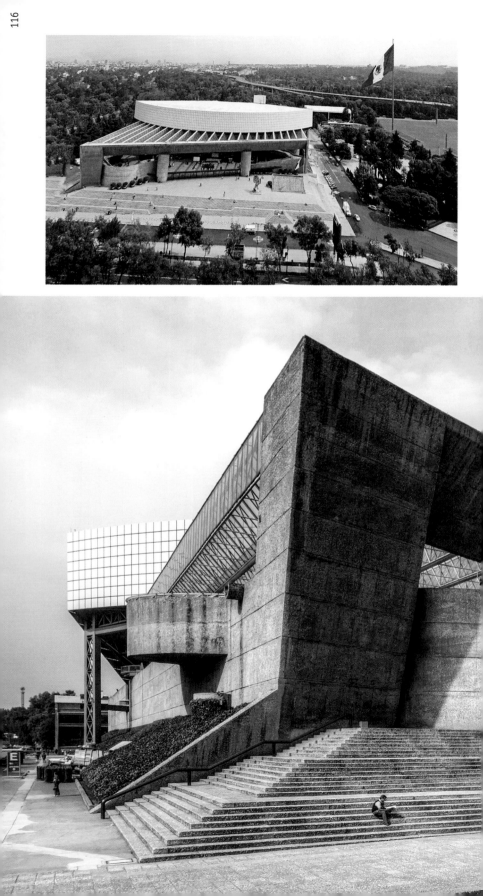

Auditorio Nacional **063 A**
Paseo de la Reforma 50,
Col. Polanco, Miguel Hidalgo
Teodoro González de León,
Abraham Zabludovsky
1952, 1991

The National Auditorium is an entertainment centre located on the boisterous Paseo de la Reforma. It was originally built in 1952 and later redesigned by the Mexican architects Abraham Zabludovsky and Teodoro González de León. Completed in 1991, its seating capacity was expanded to almost 10,000 seats, suitable to host a broad range of events: artistic and cultural exhibitions, trade fairs, political and social events, and pageants. The massive concrete frame and large round columns that support a series of glass roofs. Inside, there is a 23 × 23 m stage, for concerts and other performances. The entire auditorium rests on a platform, accessible by a wide set of 24 stairs.

Parroquia De San Agustín ≈ ⇥ 064 A
Av. Horacio 921,
Col. Polanco, Miguel Hidalgo
Unknown
1940s

Horacio 935 ≈ 065 A
Av. Horacio 935,
Col. Polanco, Miguel Hidalgo
Issac Broid, Saidée Springhall, José Castillo
2010

The San Agustín Parish was opened in the early 1940s. The materials used are stone, concrete, and marble. A cylinder with half a sphere on top seems to have been pressed into the south façade, curving it inwards, forming the church's sheltered main entrance, giving the impression of already being inside the edifice. Above the entrance patio, at the summit of the façade, sits a large stone cross. Two stone pillars, topped with bell towers support either side of the façade.

This residential complex was designed by Issac Broid, Saidée Springhall, and José Castillo. It was completed in 2010. The property consists of ten residential apartments, which have been distributed over the small perimeter of the site. A central courtyard was included to provide spaciousness and develop a transitional space between the large scale of the city and the apartments themselves. The façade is made up of wood slats, concrete, and glass windows.

Edificio Vita Polanco ⌃ ⤶ 066 A
Blvd. Miguel de Cervantes
Saavedra 171A,
Col. Polanco, Miguel Hidalgo
Archetonic
2009

The Vita Polanco building project stands
on the entire perimeter of the square site,
explaining the building's cubic shape. The
atrium, the centre of the building, ade-
quately ventilates and provides natural
light for all the dwellings. Situated on the
corner of an intersection, the design also
provides exterior views from each apartment. The façade is of concrete and glass
panels, and balconies along the entire
length of the exterior walls.

Dumas + Horacio ⌄ 067 A
Av. Horacio and Alejandro Dumas,
Col. Polanco, Miguel Hidalgo
Central de Arquitectura
2005

The Dumas and Horacio apartment buildings are situated in the Polanco neighbourhood. The building is made up of
two separate bodies of four levels each,
which are connected to one another
by a communal hallway and staircase.
A total of thirteen apartments are distributed within the two towers. One
building element accomodates for six
apartments and the other for seven. The
translucent façade uses glass blocks that
have vitroblock characteristics.

2

Tori Tori Restaurant « ≳   068 A
Temístocles 61,
Col. Polanco, Miguel Hidalgo
Rojkind Arquitectos
2009

The Tori Tori restaurant is a popular Japanese restaurant, housed in the copy of an existing residential property. The building's organic façade and landscape were carefully designed to become an extension of the restaurant, creating a strong link between the interior and exterior. The façade seems to emerge from the ground, weaves through the building and has two self-supporting layers of steel plates, cut exactly to size with a Computer Numerical Control (CNC) machine. The façade's pattern seems to change according to the interior light, shadows, and views.

Sala de Arte Siqueiros ≳   069 A
Tres Picos 29,
Col. Polanco, Miguel Hidalgo
Héctor Esrawe, a | 911,
José Castillo, Saidée Springhall
1969, 2009

The Siqueiros Art Museum displays the works of David Alfaro Siqueiros, the Mexican social realist painter, who in part established Mexican Muralism. Originally the artist's private residence, it was converted into a museum in 1969, presenting contemporary art. In 2009 Héctor Esrawe and a | 911 remodelled the 75 m² access area into a new social space that attracts visitors, for the removal of two of the existing walls on the ground floor opened the space and allows the murals to be visible from the street.

Teatro Telcel/
Cervantes Theatre ⌄ ⌐
070 A

Blvd. Miguel de Cervantes Saavedra,
Col. Ampliación Granada, Miguel Hidalgo
Ensamble Studio, Antón García Abril
2012

The Telcel/Cervantes Theatre is situated next to the Soumaya Museum, on the Carso Plaza. Completed in 2012, its design was established by Ensamble Studio, appearing as a defiance to gravity. The minimal pillars, of variable geometric shapes, which support the roof structure in a distinctive way, offer a free open space with an abstract balance. Sunlight filters through the roof's slats, thereby adding to the perceptive qualities of the weightless structure. The symbolic metal roof structure sits above an excavated open pit below, consequently extending the volume of void space. The 115,000 m² underground theatre is an example of how contemporary architecture can be inspired by the impalpable element of light.

Museo Soumaya ≈ ≽   071 A
Blvd. Miguel de Cervantes
Saavedra 303,
Col. Ampliación Granada, Miguel Hidalgo
Fernando Romero
2011

The Soumaya Museum, on Carso Plaza was designed by the renowned Mexican architect, Fernando Romero, and constructed by Carlos Slim in 2011. The avant-garde building is 46 m-high, with a seven-ring structural system. On the outside of this edifice, cladding the warped façade, are 16,000 hexagonal, silver aluminum panels. These panels look like they are hovering, for they are each separately attached to the building's structure. The asymmetric museum is structurally supported by vertical steel columns and beams, which curve with the façade. Landscaped steps lead the way to the building's narrow main entrance. Inside, tall curving white concrete walls, with an artificially lit rim, surround the foyer that is used as a gallery or exhibition space. Rounded diagonal columns support the roof structure and a white marble staircase separates the ground floor from the level above. A semi-transparent roof naturally lights the top floor, which is column-free. Furthermore, the museum contains six exhibition rooms, a library, a restaurant, and an auditorium, with a seating capacity for 320 people. The 17,000 m² museum contains close to 70,000 pieces of art, ranging from the fifteenth to the mid-twentieth centuries. The museum displays gold and silver arts, and works of European and Novo-Hispanic artists.

2

Comercio 117 «
Comercio 117,
Col. Escandón, Miguel Hidalgo
Archetonic
2012

This building is a reconfiguration of the existing 1950s building, which was previously used as a storage facility. This structure serves as a supporting base for the new, 18-apartment residential complex; a low cost development that utilises simple, strong, and low-cost materials, which correspond to the housing programme. The light, glazed façade allows for views towards the interior spaces, all the while providing security, and allowing sunlight to enter the building.

Museo Jumex ≈
Blvd. Miguel de Cervantes Saavedra 303,
Col. Ampliación Granada, Miguel Hidalgo
David Chipperfield
2013

This 4,000 m² art museum exhibits permanent and temporary, national and international art. Designed by the British architect David Chipperfield, its characteristic sawtooth roof forms the angled skylights, which light the top floor. The museum includes office and meeting spaces on the lower level, and is centred around a main staircase made of black steel panels with travertine steps; its walls are of unpolished white concrete.

EF + CG Showroom ≈
Campos Elíseos 158,
Col. Polanco, Miguel Hidalgo
Ezequiel Farca + Cristina Grappin
2015

The showroom belonging to the architects Ezequiel Farca and Cristina Grappin presents itself as a cubic, plant-like element with a green wall that covers the upper levels. The street entrance has a concrete finish, the primary architectural element. The interior space exhibits the architects' projects and ideology, and integrates the design studio. The furnishings are simple and practical, designed to facilitate and inspire the best possible collaboration amongst designers.

2

Embajada de Alemania
(German Embassy)
Av. Horacio 1506,
Col. Polanco, Miguel Hidalgo
Staab Architekten
2006

The interpretation of local building traditions and the integration of the built environment are important notions that help put a building into its urban context; these are key features of the European architectural tradition, and a fundamental theme for the new German Embassy in Mexico City. It was designed by Staab Architekten, its construction was supervised by Nuño Mac Gregor y de Buen Arquitectos. This establishment has a constructed surface of 3,472 m, comprising two floors above ground and one underground level. The compound is developed around three courtyards, whose enclosing walls are both the boundary wall and the façade of the building. The first is visible from the street and serves as an entry plaza, accessible to vehicles and visitors, once they have gone through security. This gives the embassy a certain open aspect and direct rapport with its neighbouring buildings. The other two enclosed courtyards – respectively on the east and west sides of the property – are reserved for the German embassy staff and official events. These outdoor spaces are shielded from public access by walls that extend to the street. In addition to their protective function with their formal generosity and abstraction, they give a face to the embassy. However, large windows at the centre of the street-side walls of the courtyards let the passers-by enjoy the view of these singular spaces. All of the offices and waiting rooms look out onto one of these courtyards, whose vertical and horizontal surfaces are clad with a light-coloured, marble-like natural stone – as are the compound walls that give onto the streets. The street-front façades of the embassy, however, use tezontle – an endemic red lava stone – also used for the construction of many historic and contemporary buildings in Mexico City. The central lobby, which opens onto all three courtyards, shares its natural light with the adjacent rooms and circulation spaces, rendering the inside spatial organisation of the embassy fluid and coherent to its users. The interior decoration – hues of green and gold, and the wooden interior furniture, floors, staircases, and ledges – lends a modest, quite intimate atmosphere to the whole.

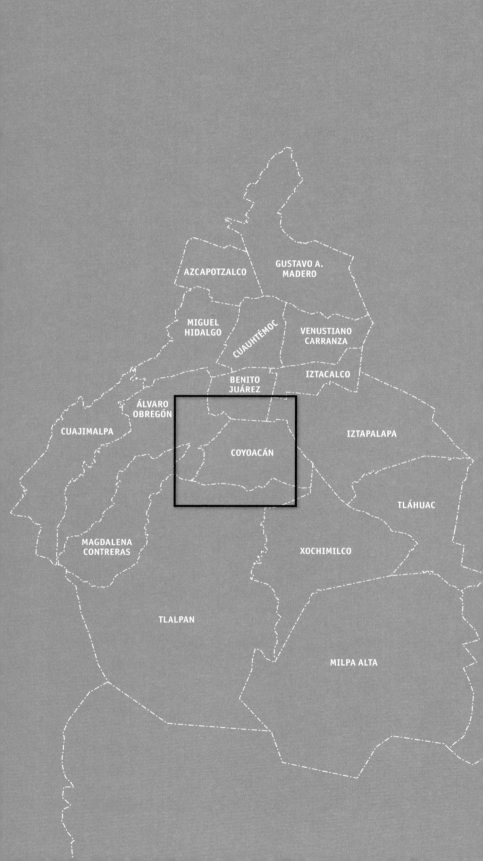

Inside the UNAM: The Largest University in Latin America

Inside the UNAM: The Largest University in Latin America

The Universidad Nacional Autónoma de México (the National Autonomous University of Mexico – more commonly known as the UNAM) is one of the most recognised universities in Latin America and the Spanish-speaking world in general. The Ciudad Universitaria (University City) – the UNAM's main campus – is located in Coyoacán, the southern part of Mexico City. Designed by some of the leading Mexican architects of the twentieth century, such as Mario Pani and Enrique del Moral, the University City was built on an ancient solidified lava bed called *El Pedregal,* covering a surface of 7.3 km². Construction was completed in 1954 at a cost of ca. 25 million USD. At the time of its completion, it was the largest, single construction project in the entire country of Mexico since the Aztecs. It is also one of the largest and most architecturally celebrated campuses, featuring modern Latin American architecture. It encloses the Olympic Stadium, about 40 faculties and institutes, the Cultural Centre, an ecological reserve, the Central Library, and a few museums. Furthermore, as the buildings are highly artistically detailed – murals in the main campus were painted by some of the most recognized artists in Mexican history, such as Diego Rivera and David Alfaro Siqueiros – the university campus was declared a UNESCO World Heritage site in 2007. In 2015, the entire UNAM infrastructure had a total of 2,180 buildings (comprising 4,576 classrooms, 4,088 offices, and 2,824 laboritories), over 12 thousand full-time employees, and over 340,000 students.

Source: Martin Wimmel Archive

Site plan

Torre II de Humanidades ⌃ `076` B
Av. Universidad 3000,
Col. Ciudad Universitaria, Coyoacán
Mario Pani
1952

The Torre II de Humanidades was designed by the Mexican architect Mario Pani and completed in 1952, at the same time as several other buildings on campus. The tower is 56 m tall, with sixteen levels, twelve of which primarily serve as office space. The building is located next to the Alfonso Caso Auditorium on one of the many large plazas on the UNAM campus. The building's façade consists of an outer frame of red concrete blocks, enclosing strips of glazed windows, set in a tight aluminium grid.

Facultad de Medicina » `077` B
Av. Universidad 3000,
Col. Ciudad Universitaria, Coyoacán
Roberto Álvarez Espinoza et al.
1952

Designed by Roberto Álvarez Espinoza, Pedro Ramírez Vázquez, Ramón Torres Martínez, and Héctor Velázquez, the Faculty of Medicine stands in the centre of the UNAM campus. The building is composed of seven separate entities. A large ceramic mural, by Francisco Eppens Helguera covers the curved façade of an entire wall (20 × 18 m). This distinctive architectural feature is visible from a distance and is a representation of a cosmological conception of Mexico's indigenous ancestors and the four elements.

3

Biblioteca Central UNAM 078 B

Campus Central de la UNAM,
Col. Ciudad Universitaria, Coyoacán
Juan O'Gorman, Gustavo María Saavedra,
Juan Martínez de Velasco
1956

The UNAM Central Library large cuboid form is set on a platform 3 m above the rest of the terrain, elevating it and making it a central landmark of the university campus. The 16,000 m² library has 10 floors. The façade murals are mosaics made from millions of coloured tiles from all around Mexico. The north side pictures Mexico's pre-Hispanic past and the south facade its colonial one, while the east wall depicts the contemporary world, and the west shows the university and contemporary Mexico.

3

Auditorio Alfonso Caso

Av. Universidad 3000,
Col. Ciudad Universitaria
Raúl Cacho, Eugenio Peschard,
Félix Sánchez
1953

Completed in 1953, the Alfonso Caso Auditorium displays a mural by José Chávez Morado, called the Conquest of Energy, on the facade of its northern wall. This composition symbolises Man's struggle to find a vital source after the discovery of fire. This portion of the façade is clad in metal sheets and the remaining materials consist of concrete and glass. The southern roof of the building's long geometric form is broken into wave-like sections.

Pabellón De Rayos Cósmicos ≈ `080` `B`
Av. Universidad 3000,
Col. Ciudad Universitaria, Coyoacán
Félix Candela
1951

The Pavilion of Cosmic Rays is located inside the UNAM campus. The mathematically complex structure explores parabolic forms. Its double-curved vault construction provides structural strength, stability, and simplicity of design. The pavilion houses two laboratories, through which cosmic rays are able to pass, due to the thin innovative concrete structure. Elevated off the ground, like a space-ship, reinforced concrete stairs lead to the lobby within. This floating staircase is supported on only one side and does not include a balustrade.

Estadio Olímpico `081` `B`
Universitario ≈ »
Av. Insurgentes Sur s/n,
Col. Ciudad Universitaria, Coyoacán
Augusto Pérez Palacios, Raúl Salinas Moro, Jorge Bravo Jiménez
1952

The University Stadium was already opened in 1952 and used sixteen years later for the 1968 Olympic Games. Today the sporting facility is home to the UNAM *Los Pumas* Football club, and can seat about 70,000 spectators. The stadium was designed to immitate a volcanic crater. Its decorative exterior at the main entrance is a stone mosaic created by the artist Diego Rivera. This mural depicts Mexican athletes, the huge plumed serpent and the Aztec god, Quetzalcóatl.

Source: Martin Wimmer, Stadium Buildings, Berlin 2016

The Olympic Stadium as an Architectural Masterpiece of Latin American Modernism

Inka Humann

Mexico City was awarded the Olympic Games in 1968. So far, this honour had always been allocated to countries with a great sporting tradition. At the time, Mexico only had professional boxing, football and bullfighting to show for. Mexico's famous architect, Pedro Ramírez Vázquez, was appointed President of the Organising Committee. He planned the extensive Olympic construction program, and organised, amongst others, the conversion of the Olympic University stadium with about 60,000 seats. Vázquez initiated a novelty in the Olympic Games: nineteen artistic competitions (including architecture), as equivalents to the nineteen athletic competitions. For the first time, an all-weather tartan track was used for the running events, instead of the existing cinder track. In terms of urban development, the integration of the dispersed sports facilities into one of the world's largest metropolis was certainly a problem, regarding chaotic traffic. Likewise, the extreme altitude of the city – at 2,265 m above sea level – caused warning voices concerning the physical strain on the athletes, due to lower oxygen levels. But despite the additional political and medical difficulties, the games were played out and were even very successful. The architects in charge of the stadium on the campus of the National Autonomous University of Mexico were Augusto Pérez Palacios, Raúl Salinas Moro, and Jorge Bravo Jiménez. Previously used in the 1950s and the 1960s, as a venue for American football games at the university, it was transformed into an Olympic Stadium, with an increased capacity, in 1968. In the southwest of the city, this modern-style stadium was the largest stadium in Mexico. A part of the building was lowered to the same level as its surroundings, which facilitated access to the seats on the two grandstand levels. Furthermore, no staircases were required in the outdoor area. Inspired by the shape of a volcanic crater, the stadium is a successful example of its integration into the surrounding landscape. The use of endemic lava rock as a building material, gives this stadium an almost organic appearance. On the longitudinal sides of the building, on a elliptic floorplan, the exterior walls and thus the grandstands, are higher than on the transverse sides, resulting in an ondulating silhouette. In this manner, the stadium combines beauty of form with economic factors. To achieve a synthesis of architecture and fine art, the outer wall of the stadium was supposed to be decorated with a large mosaic of coloured stone, by the Mexican artist Diego Rivera; the title of the mural was: *the University, the Mexican Family, Peace, and Youth Sports*. Unfortunately, the project remained unfinished due to the artist's death and the lack of financial resources. Yet, the special architectural and artistic design integrates this saddle-shaped stadium complex, in the landscape of Mexico City.

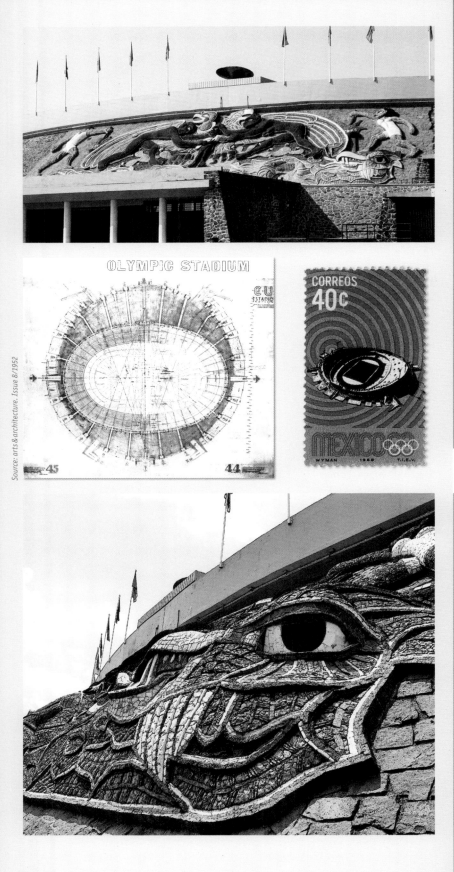

OLYMPIC STADIUM

CORREOS 40c

MEXICO68

WYMAN 1968 T.I.E.V.

Source: arts & architecture. Issue 8/1952

Selected Olympic Stadiums 1912–2012

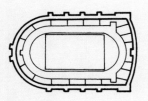

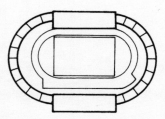

**Olympic Stadium, Stockholm
(Olympic Games, 1912)**
Completion: 1912, capacity: 14,500
Architect: Torben Grut
The floor plan of the Olympic Stadium is based on the horse-shoe shape with a feature wall and is defined by two towers.

**Olympic Stadium, Amsterdam
(Olympic Games, 1928)**
Completion: 1928, capacity: 22,000
Architect: Jan Wills
This stadium intergrated the last ever velodrome into an Olympic Stadium, due to 400 m tracks becoming mandatory.

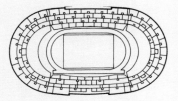

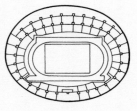

**Stadio Olimpico, Rome
(Olympic Games, 1960)**
Completion: 1937, capacity: 73,000
Architect: Annibale Vitellozzi
The Olympic Stadium's floor plan took a unique longitudinal form and its seating was distributed across three tiers.

**Olympic Stadium, Tokyo
(Olympic Games, 1964)**
Completion: 1958, capacity: 57,000
Architect: Mitsuo Katayama
The floor plan is of circular form and contains two long asymmetrical sides internally alongside the playing field.

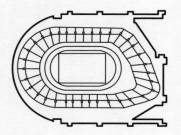

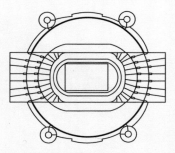

**Centennial Stadium, Atlanta
(Olympic Games, 1996)**
Completion: 1996, capacity: 85,000
Architect: Heery International et al.
The stadium's unique form was designed in such a way, to later be converted into a baseball stadium.

**ANZ Stadium, Sydney
(Olympic Games, 2000)**
Completion: 1999, Architects: Bligh Lobb Sports Architects, Populous
The Sydney stadium rises from a circular floor plan; the grandstands were able to be dismantled after the Olympic Games.

Source: Martin Wimmer, Stadium Buildings. Construction and Design Manual. Berlin 2016

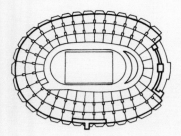

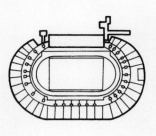

Memorial Coliseum, Los Angeles (Olympic Games, 1932)
Completion: 1923, capacity: 93,600
Architects: J & D Parkinson
The Memorial Coliseum's floor plan design was based on an elliptical shape as a starting point for construction.

Olympic Stadium, Helsinki (Olympic Games, 1952)
Completion: 1938, capacity: 40,682
Architects: Yrjö Lindegren, Toivo Jäntti
The stadium's floor plan is of small elliptical form and features a tower on the southern end of the main arena.

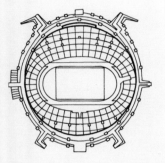

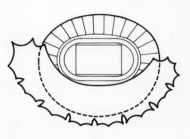

Estadio Universitario, Mexico City (Olympic Games, 1968)
Completion: 1952, capacity: 63,150
Architects: Augusto Pérez Palacios et al.
The stadium is of circular shape with distinctive asymmetrical and saddle-shaped grandstands.

Olympiastadion, Munich (Olympic Games, 1972)
Completion: 1972, capacity: 69,250
Architects: Behnisch & Partner et al.
The stadium is circular in form, with asymmetrical grandstands, of which a majority of the seats are covered.

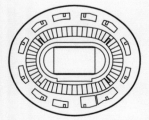

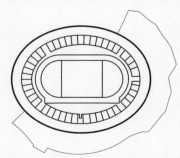

National Stadium, Beijing (Olympic Games, 2008)
Completion: 2008, capacity: 90,000
Architects: Herzog & de Meuron
The stadium's form is based on an oval floor plan and its façade consists of complex external intertwined lines.

Olympic Stadium, London (Olympic Games, 2012)
Completion: 2011, reconstruction: 2016, capacity: 60,000, future capacity: 54,000
Architects: Populous, Buro Happold
The Olympic Stadium is of oval form and contains three tiers.

3

Biblioteca y Hemeroteca   082 B
Centro Cultural Universitario,
Col. Ciudad Universitaria, Coyoacán
Orso Núñez Ruiz Velasco et. al.
1976

The National Library is also located within the UNAM campus at the University Cultural Center. The exterior cladding of the building comprises a vast amount of concrete blocks as well as large glass windows. Triangular concrete canopies extend at an angle from the buildings façade and a wide set of stairs lead to the library's main entrance. The National Library's consulting rooms contain encyclopedias, dictionaries, and books on a variety of topics.

Edificio de la Torre de Rectoría 083 B
Campus Central de la UNAM,
Col. Ciudad Universitaria, Coyoacán
Mario Pani, Enrique del Moral,
Salvador Ortega Flores
1980

Designed by Mario Pani, Enrique del
Moral, and Salvador Ortega, the administration tower is situated across from the
UNAM stadium at the centre of the university campus. The building consists of
geometric forms, and the tower itself has
protruding elements, one in particular
being a circulation shaft. The building's
façade is of marble and glass with various, large, three dimensional murals by
David Alfaro Siqueiros.

3

Museo Universitario Arte Contemporáneo

Av. de Los Insurgentes Sur 3000,
Col. Ciudad Universitaria, Coyoacán
Teodoro González de León
2008

The University Contemporary Art Museum is located at the far south of the UNAM campus; this social and cultural institution exhibits national and international contemporary art. Designed by mexican architect Teodoro González de León, this two-level building has a total of 14,000 m². Inside, there are conference rooms, an auditorium, a restaurant, a store, and temporary exhibition rooms. The museum is mostly a flat concrete structure. However, the sloped, glazed wall of the main entrance is built at a steep angle. The entrance patio is covered by a series of beams, which project angled shadows, creating a continuum of the angled façade.

3

Biblioteca de la Facultad de Medicina UNAM 085 B

Av. Universidad 3000,
Col. Ciudad Universitaria, Coyoacán
Nuño Mac Gregor De Buen Arquitectos
2007

The new extension building for the Library of the Faculty of Medicine is located at the northeast corner of the UNAM campus. Nuño Mac Gregor De Buen Arquitectos designed the expansion and renovation of the original building, which has three main bodies and ramps. Construction was completed in 2007. The library is now organised around a central, double height space, with a skylight. The main staircase and elevator are also situated at the centre of the library; in this manner, creating a natural interior light well that diffuses to the spaces around it. The basement contains several service rooms for staff. The entire library is one open space, supported by medium-sized concrete pillars. Shelves and glass partitions aim to create the perception of a fully transparent structure. The exterior is made up of large glass panels with exposed concrete structural elements. The library also has a roof terrace, which is accessible to students, and offers views over the campus. The study rooms are shielded from sunlight by trees that are planted at the basement level.

3

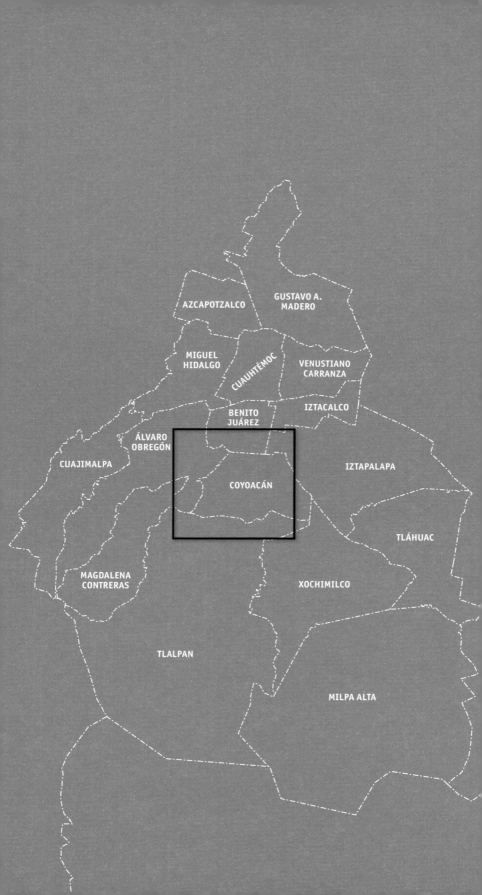

Around the UNAM: Cultural and Residential Districts

Around the UNAM: Cultural and Residential Districts

Álvaro Obregón and Cuajimalpa de Morelos are located in the far west of Mexico City. The Tlalpan district forms a portion of the south and is home to the frequently visited Azteca Stadium. They are all highly residential areas. The Benito Juárez and Coyoacán districts are prominantly populated by the upper middle class. The Coyoacán district is where the celebrated artists Frida Kahlo and Diego Rivera lived during the early twentieth century. Many of its cobblestone streets connect to several public parks and squares. Various educational institutions and campuses can be found in both districts.

092 B

Source: Martin Wimmer Archive

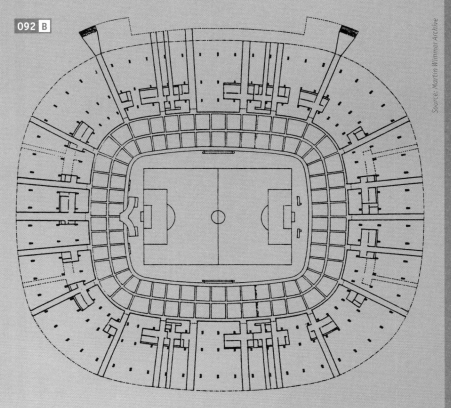

Estadio Azteca, floor plan (1966)

4

Museo Frida Kahlo ≈   086 B
Londres 247,
Col. del Carmen, Coyoacán
Unknown
19th century

The celebrated Frida Kahlo Museum, also known as La Casa Azul (the Blue House) – for the cobalt-blue exterior (and interior) walls – is one of Mexico City's most visited attractions. It sits on the corner of Londres and Allende in the Coyoacán district and was built in 1904. Originally home of the late Mexican artist, Frida Kahlo, it was transformed into a museum by her husband, Diego Rivera, to exhibit their work and private Mexican artefacts. The two-storey, 800m² property also encloses a central courtyard of another 400m², with a lush garden, a traditional colonial architectural layout.

Casa Negro y Mila ⌐ ≈   087 B
Address unknown
Coyoacán
*Rozana Montiel Estudio de Arquitectura,
Viviana Martínez Negrete*
2004

The Negro and Mila House is a low budget, 90 m², two-level, residential project, in the backyard of a pre-existing residence. The house was built around the 12 m tall trunk of a live Ash tree. This creates a small patio at the centre of the building. Thanks to the height of the tree and its canopy that spreads out over the rooftop, the dwelling is naturally ventilated and lit from within, for the interior also has large windows that give onto the lightwell. The building is mainly constructed of sand-coloured concrete bricks and large iron-framed windows.

Hera 24

Av. Hera,
Col. Crédito Constructor, Benito Juárez
dmp arquitectura, Carlos Díaz Delgado,
Carlos Díaz San Pedro
2012

The Hera 24 residential building is located in the Benito Juárez district. The building's design is strongly influenced by the singular shape of the site: two different blocks, which are connected to a vertical circulation core. This housing complex contains seven apartments, each with their unique spatial arrangements, therefore targeting a wider clientele. The building's structure consists of load-bearing walls and concrete waffle slabs, thus eliminating the need for columns and increasing spatial circulation. The entire building is naturally lit and ventilated. The main façade is covered with plants, which are irrigated with a system of recycled rainwater that is collected at the foot of the building.

4

Revolución Apartments

Revolución 534,
Col. San Pedro de los Pinos, Benito Juárez
SLOT Studio
2012

The original structure of Revolución Apartments is from the 1960's. It was extended and redesigned in 2012, with a new 9-storey building on a neighbouring plot, creating a budget-sensitive, commercially attractive, and socially appealing living-space. This complex comprises 48 apartments, ranging from 110 m² to 140 m² each, and ground-floor retail. Being on a corner location highly influenced the building's shape: the two exterior façades provide great views from within. The multiple protruding angles accentuate the depth of the building's atypical, horizontal composition, which integrates a rhythm of vertical brise-soleil slats.

Elena Garro Cultural Center

Fernández Leal 43,
Col. La Concepción, Coyoacán
Fernanda Canales, a | 911
2013

The Elena Garro Cultural Center integrates a heritage-listed house into a contemporary architectural project, and transforms it into a multi-purpose cultural centre. The original building is incorporated and encased between two new elements (predominantly concrete and glazing); extending and sheltering it on three sides, yet opening it to the street, by the means of a wide glass wall. The façade of the old house, and its contemporary extension become the central element of the design, and are dedicated to the library. A void has been left in the ceiling of the front extension, allowing one of the existing trees to pass through, turning it into a feature element. This void also serves as a skylight, filling the space with natural light. Both new architectural elements are connected by an interior bridge, and they have been grafted to the existing house in such a way that has no direct impact on its structure.

4

Cineteca Nacional   091 B

Av. México Coyoacán 389,
Col. Xoco, Benito Juárez
Rojkind Arquitectos
Ongoing

Located in the southern district of
Mexico City, the National Film Archive
and Film Institute of Mexico is home to
the most important film heritage of Latin
America. Today's building is an expansion
and renovation of the existing complex.
The public plaza is sheltered from the
weather by a hovering canopy, connecting the existing complex with the new
screening rooms. Cladded in composite
aluminium panels, with various-sized triangular perforations, the roof structure
wraps around the new screening rooms,
thus forming the façade. The sheltered
space functions as the foyer for the old
and new screening rooms, and accom-
modates for concerts, theatres, exhibitions, etc. An outdoor amphitheatre,
extensive landscaping, and new retail
spaces were added to the original programme, expanding the possibilities for
social and cultural interaction. Overall,
the complex can seat up to 2,495 visitors
in its indoor theatres.

Source: Hennes Weisweiler, IX. Fußball Weltmeisterschaft Mexico 1970. Gütersloh 1970

Estadio Azteca 092 B

Calzada de Tlalpan 3465,
Col. Santa Úrsula Coapa, Coyoacán
Pedro Ramírez Vázquez,
Rafael Mijares Alcérreca
1968

The subsequent stages of the stadium revolution took place in Latin America with the construction of the Maracanã football stadium (officially known as Estádio Jornalista Mário Filho) in Rio de Janeiro for the 1950 football World Cup, and the construction of the Aztec football stadium in Mexico City in 1968. At that time, Brazil and Mexico were amongst the poorest countries of the world. Nevertheless, they were the first to introduce completely roofed-over stands all around the stadium: in one country for 200,000 spectators, and in the other for 110,000; the latter has cantilever roofs. If the Estádio do Maracanã was the largest football stadium in the world prior to its reconstruction – involving a reduced spectator capacity – the Estadio Azteca is still amongst the world elite of stadiums today, both functionally and aesthetically: it has a capacity of 105,000 spectators – 80 per cent of the seats are sheltered. The 1962 design was elaborated by the Mexican architects Pedro Ramírez Vázquez and Rafael Mijares Alcérreca. Today, the Estadio Azteca is home to the professional football team Club América, but holds concerts and other major events as well.

Source: Deutsche Bauzeitung (Germany). Issue 7/1970

4

Liverpool Insurgentes ⌃   `093` `B`
Av. Insurgentes Sur 1310,
Col. del Valle, Tlalpan
Rojkind Arquitectos
2012

The Liverpool department store is a single box body, wrapped in a graphically intricate envelope. This 2.80 m deep façade not only serves as an awning, providing pedestrians with shelter; it is also accessible from inside – through large openings – providing space for various temporary displays. The light which emanates from and reflects off of this porous façade (a three-layered hexagon system, made of fiberglass, steel, aluminium, and glass) gives the building a lantern-like expression, making it an urban beacon.

Museo Casa Estudio de   `094` `B`
Diego Rivera y Frida Kahlo »
Calle Diego Rivera 2,
Col. San Ángel, Álvaro Obregón
Juan O'Gorman
1931

This building, opened to the public in 1986 as a museum, was designed to provide separate living quarters and studio spaces for the renowned Mexican artists. The two blocks are connected by a small bridge on the top level, metaphorically expressing the love connecting the spouses. The 380 m² site also includes a third entity, containing a photography laboratory. The sawtooth roof of the red and white body represents the Mexican working class, to which Diego Rivera felt connected.

Corporativo IBM

095 B

Av. Vasco de Quiroga and Joaquín Gallo,
Col. Zedec Santa Fe, Álvaro Obregón
Nuño Mac Gregor De Buen Arquitectos
1997

The IBM Corporate building is a five-level building in the shape of a semi-trapezoidal concrete and glass body of 25,000 m². Its base covers 7,500 m². It is encased approximately 2 m below street level, and surrounded by a partly terraced garden. This 100 m long office building is divided in two at the centre-front façade, by a reception lobby that reaches up to the fourth level. This hall is encased in glass and enables natural light to enter the establishment, diffusing towards the adjacent spaces. The elevators, main staircase, and other services, are all concentrated in this central space. The top level is slightly recessed from the main façade, providing space for balconies and large bay windows. The building offers spatial flexibility, economical operation, and an identifiable image.

Corporativo Banorte » 096 B
Av. Prolongación Reforma 1230,
Col. Lomas de Santa Fe, Álvaro Obregón
Arditti + RDT Arquitectos
2013

The Banorte Coporate tower is located on the Paseo de la Reforma. The building is limited to a maximum height of 40 levels according to Reforma regulations and a restricted façade of only 16 m. The building has a total constructed surface of 33,800 m² and towers 140 m above street level. The initial project was to highlight three levels with three different bodies, which assembled, form the shape of the building. These consist of a slim twenty-seven-level tower and a mezzanine that seems pushed out of the general volumetric, providing a ludic effect to the verticality of the building.

4

Casa Tes 097 B
Tesoreros 58,
Col. Toriello Guerra, Tlalpan
Nuño Mac Gregor De Buen Arquitectos
2000

The Tes House is a residential home, located in Tlalpan. The building is essentially made of red brick and black metal. Its L-shape composition is due to its advantageous corner location. Its surface of 350 m² is distributed over two levels. The living space is composed of alternating geometric volumes. There are minimal openings on the street-side façades. The ground-floor commons and first-floor private spaces are connected by a double-height lobby, served by a staircase and walkway with white railing.

Falcón Headquarters 2 « 098 B

José de Teresa 188,
Col. San Ángel, Álvaro Obregón
Rojkind Arquitectos
2012

The new building was conceptualised as an extension of the existing Falcón I headquarters garden, preserving its vegetated views and emphasizing the visual connection between inside and outside. The new building was placed directly behind the yellow glass box of Falcón I, in the form of a simple transparent rectangular box. The vegetation is carried onto the glass curtain façade with modular planters, arranged in an offset linear configuration. The green wall merges into the interior through double-height atriums. A bridge connects the new rooftop park to a recently added employee dining hall, placed atop the existing building.

Chedraui Santa Fe ☆ 099 B

Av. Vasco de Quiroga 3800,
Col. Lomas de Santa Fe,
Cuajimalpa de Morelos
Rojkind Arquitectos
2013

The Chedraui store in Santa Fe has a unique appearance that incorporates a rooftop terrace on which is planted a 1,725 m² orchard. A series of pathways, connect it to a 1,230 m² market square. This space can also be used as an event platform where local community groups and schools can hold educational programs, workshops, farm tours, children's events, and so forth. The façade is composed of fiberglass-reinforced concrete panels, which give the store its very dynamic signature, contrasting with the typical *retail boxes* that have sprung up all around the neighbourhood.

4

Xomali 153

Xomali 153,
Col. San Lorenzo Huipulco, Tlalpan
dmp arquitectura
2016

The residential home was designed by dmp arquitectura, consisting of Carlos Díaz Delgado and Carlos Díaz San Pedro. The restricted 35 m² surface of land, on which the project was developed, allowed for a minimal floor plate. The ground floor includes a kitchen, a living room, a dining area, and a double height study. The second level contains a mezzanine space and the master bedroom. The building itself is a concrete structure painted in black and white. Small square windows have been scattered all over the façade, allowing light to enter the home, all the while maintaining privacy.

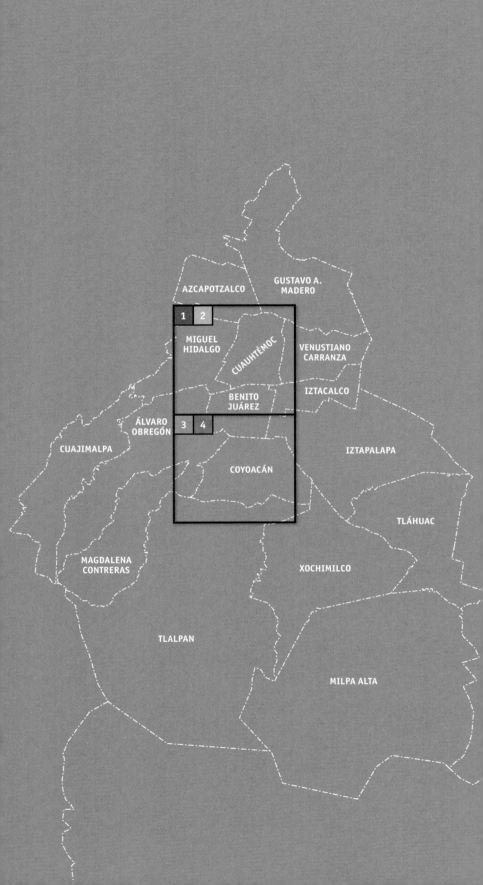

Appendix

A

| 1 | Cuauhtémoc: Historical Centre and Close Landmarks |
| 2 | West of Cuauhtémoc: Commercial and Diplomatic Districts |

AZCAPOTZALCO

Parque Bicentenario

Refinería

Egipto

Panteón Español

Panteones

Tacuba

Calzada

Avenida Ricardo Flores Magón

Cuitláhuac

México-Tacuba

Popotla

Calz. Legaria

Panteón Frances

Felipe Carrillo Puerto

Colegio Militar

055

Instituto Técnico Industrial

Eje 1 Nor

Lago Chiem

San Joaquín

Laguna de Términos

Marina Nacional

Normal

058

CIRCUITO INTERIOR

San Cosme

Avenida Río San Joaquín

070

071   072   066

Avenida Ejército Nacional

MIGUEL HIDALGO

Av. Ejército Nacional Oriente

Calzada General Mariano Escobedo

Thiers

Parque Vía

Río Tiber

029

057   064

075   059   067

065

Presidente Masaryk   061

Polanco

074   069

Circuito Interior Melchor Ocampo

044

031   030

035

046

Paseo de la Reforma

017   Insurgentes

049

Insurgentes Sur

Autopista Urbana Norte

062

068   060

063

Auditorio   Paseo de la Reforma

054

Avenida Chapultepec

Sevilla

Bosque de Chapultepec

Circuito Bicentenario

Chapultepec

033

045

Bosques

Avenida Constituyentes

Juanacatlán

050

Querета

Parque México

Panteón de Dolores

Avenida Constituyentes

Constituyentes

Avenida de los

036   039

034   Chilpancingo

056

Tamaulipas

Av. Nuevo-León

Patriotismo

Tacubaya

073

Observatorio

Viaducto Pdte. Miguel Alemán

Xola

De la Curva

Canaria

CIRCUITO INTERIOR

San Pedro de los Pinos

Viaducto Río de Becerra

Avenida de los Insurgentes Sur

Avenida División del Norte

0   1 km

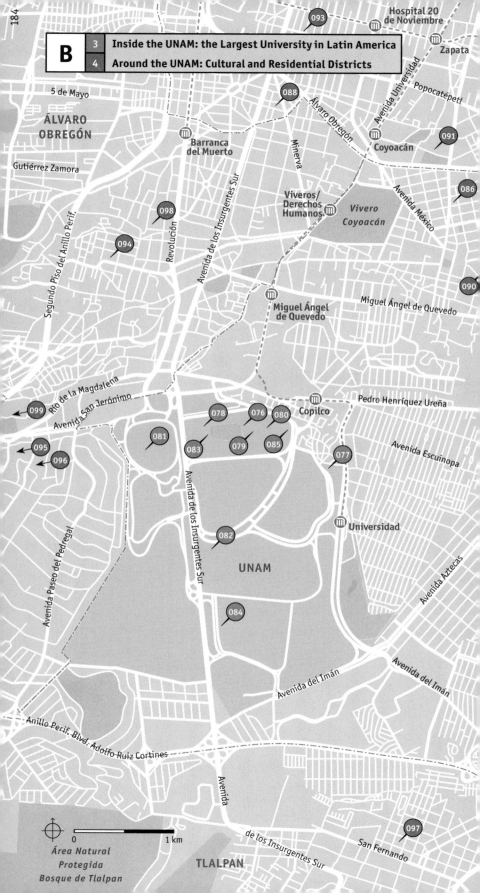

B

3 Inside the UNAM: the Largest University in Latin America

4 Around the UNAM: Cultural and Residential Districts

Hospital 20
de Noviembre

Zapata

Popocatépetl

Avenida Universidad

5 de Mayo

ÁLVARO
OBREGÓN

Barranca
del Muerto

088

Álvaro Obregón

Minerva

Coyoacán

091

Gutiérrez Zamora

Avenida de los Insurgentes Sur

Viveros/
Derechos
Humanos

Vivero
Coyoacán

Avenida México

086

Segundo Piso del Anillo Perif.

Revolución

098

094

Miguel Ángel
de Quevedo

Miguel Ángel de Quevedo

090

Río de la Magdalena

Avenida San Jerónimo

099

Pedro Henríquez Ureña

Copilco

Avenida Escuinopa

095

096

081

078

083

076

079

080

085

Avenida Paseo del Pedregal

Avenida de los Insurgentes Sur

077

Universidad

Avenida Aztecas

082

UNAM

084

Avenida del Imán

Avenida del Imán

Anillo Perif. Blvd. Adolfo Ruiz Cortines

Avenida

0   1 km

097

de los Insurgentes Sur

San Fernando

Área Natural
Protegida
Bosque de Tlalpan

TLALPAN

Architects Index
Digits indicate the project number, the letter corresponds to maps A or B

Buildings Index

Digits indicate the project number, the letter corresponds to maps A or B

Bibliography

Antonia Tapia, Perfiles. Dr. Álvaro
Sánchez, Más de 50 años junto a la
arquitectura. November 2010.

Carlos Calderón, El Estadio Azteca:
Historia del Coloso de Santa Úrsula.
México D.F. May 2001.

Carmen Galindo, Magdalena Galindo
Mexico City Historic Center.
México D.F. 2002.

Catálogo nacional de monumentos
históricos inmuebles Centro Histórico
(Perímetro A) Tomo III. Instituto
Nacional de Antropología e Historia,
México D.F. 1992.

David Lida, México D.F. Entonces y ahora/
Mexico City Then and Now.
México D.F. 2009.

El Palacio de Hierro abrirá totalmente
sus puertas. El Economista, issue of 28
September 2014.

Ernest Sánchez Santiró, El nuevo orden
parroquial de la Ciudad de México:
Población, etnia y territorio (1768-1777).
Universidad Nacional Autónoma de
México, p. 81. México D.F., 2004.

Felipe Garrido, Miquel Adrià, Marco
Barrera Bassols, Pablo Soler Frost,
Biblioteca Vasconcelos.
México D.F. 2007.

Guillermo Osorno, Ciudad de México,
Nueva Guía del Centro Histórico de
México. México D.F. 2011.

Humberto Ricalde, Lo mejor de lo mejor,
Arquitecturas Mexicanas 2001-2010.
México D.F. 2012.

John Noble, Lonely Planet Mexico City.
Lonely Planet Publications.
Melbourne 2000.

Jorge Alejandro Apanco, Planetario Luis
Enrique Erro. México D.F. 2009.

Luis Castañeda, Image-Machine: Félix
Candela's Palacio de los Deportes.
Pidgin Magazine, Spring 2010, pp. 246-257.

Manuel Rivera Cambas,
México Pintoresco, Artístico y
Monumental. México D.F. 1967.

Martin Wimmer, Construction and Design
Manual: Stadium Buildings.
DOM publishers, Berlin 2016.

Michael J. Lazzara, Vicky Unruh, Telling
Ruins in Latin America.
New York City 2009.

Rafael Cal, Mayor Leach, Iglesias del
Centro Histórico de la Ciudad de México.
México D.F. 2011.

Richard Nebel, Santa María Tonantzin
Virgen de Guadalupe. México D.F. 1995.

Sandro, Landucci Lerdo de Tejada,
Estadio Azteca 40 años. México D.F. 2006.
Palacio de Bellas Artes. Mexico City:
Secretary of Tourism of Mexico.
México D.F. 2005.

Thomas Benjamin, La Revolución:
Mexico's Great Revolution as Memory,
Myth, and History. Austin: University of
Texas Press, 2000.

Toyo Ito, Víctor Jiménez, Xavier Guzmán
Urbiola, Casa O'Gorman 1929.
México D.F. March 2015.

Author and Co-Authors

Sarah Zahradnik, born in Germany, graduated from the University of South Australia with a Masters degree in Architecture. Since then, she has worked in architectural offices in Australia, Brazil, Mexico, and Germany. She speaks four languages and has sold her designs for residential houses in Mexico. Sarah is currently writing her third book, Architectural Guide, Australia, and is also working as a Project Architect in Melbourne, Australia.

Adlai Pulido, born in Mexico, graduated from the Universidad Nacional Autónoma de México. He studied the relationship between art and architecture and has been published in design magazines.

Inka Humann, born in Fulda, Germany, studied art history in Marburg and Berlin, and graduated with a thesis on the works of the German visual artist Gerhard Richter. Since 2013 works as a publishing editor for *DOM publishers*.

Photo Credits

The *Deutsche Nationalbibliothek* lists this publication in the *Deutsche Nationalbibliografie*; detailed bibliographic data are available on the Internet at http://dnb.d-nb.de.

ISBN 978-3-86922-374-2

© 2017 by DOM publishers, Berlin
www.dom-publishers.com

Final Proofreading
Laura Thépot

Design
Sarah Zahradnik

Final Artwork
Lupe Bezzina

Maps
Katrin Soschinski

Printing
Tiger Printing (Hong Kong) Co., Ltd.
www.tigerprinting.hk